ASTRO—COMPATIBILITY

by

Gail "Ariel" Guttman

RKM PUBLISHING CO.
Euclid, Ohio

RKM PUBLISHING CO.
P.O. Box 23042
Euclid, OH 44123

Printed in the United States of America by
Book Crafters, Chelsea, Michigan.

First Printing: June, 1986

Cover Design: Eric C. Bloom

ISBN 0-87500-020-7

TABLE OF CONTENTS

ACKNOWLEDGEMENTS

There are numerous people who helped me on the road to completion of this manuscript. I suppose I should start with Norm Flynn who gave me the unlimited use of his Apple computer to begin typing the manuscript way before I knew what a control character was. Then there were all the friends, teachers and students along the way who helped in numerous informational ways. The editors whose careful reading of the manuscript and sensitive comments assisted me in communicating my information a little more clearly were Penny Hill, Grace Yount, Nancy Lattier and Sharon Morrison-Fletter and I sincerely thank them. Carmela Corallo was there all along the way with the utmost of support and caring. But above all, there's Michael, whose endless patience, thoughtful teaching and quiet knowing has given me the strength to make it happen.

FOREWARD

As Man moves into the New Age, his most important actions will be taken in relationships. Gail Guttman has done her part to help move Man into the New Age by helping people understand how they interrelate with one another. As Gail mentions later in this book, each of the planets has transited through the sign of relationships, Libra, over the past century. Each planet has shed a different light on this sign, expanding our awareness of relationships. Pluto made its last transit of Libra in August, 1984; with this book, Gail gives us the first look at relationships as we enter this new developmental cycle.

ASTRO-COMPATIBILITY is the most comprehensive book on relationships I have ever read. Gail gives you her years of knowledge and research written in a fast, easy-to-read style made enjoyable by her thoroughness. This, I am sure, is the first of many books that will come from Gail.

Robert "Buz" Myers

LIST OF ILLUSTRATIONS

INTRODUCTION

WHY RELATIONSHIPS?

My personal belief is we experience richer, more reward-
ing lives when we share who we are with another. I believe in love and in pairing. This involves relationships -
of all kinds.

People everywhere are trying to make the most of relationships by exploring all the alternatives offered today.
Dating services, singles' bars, talk shows, books, maga-
zines and seminars are thriving by focusing on relationships, marriage and divorce. Never before have so many
people sought to understand their role and their partners'
role. Before the 1950's, it was unlikely that you would
change partners or even have the opportunity to choose if
you wanted a life-time partner. Society said you needed
marriage to be happy. Society said you must marry and you
did. That is no longer the case today. People have a
choice now. Instead of marrying once and staying that way,
people are postponing marriage and/or marrying several
times in the course of a lifetime.

My purpose in this book is twofold. The first is to
help each of us clarify and understand what we are looking
for in relationships. The second is to help us feel we are
fulfilling our needs once we are involved in relationships,
thereby creating peace and harmony within ourselves.

In analyzing these needs, it is best to keep in mind
that we are not trying to remake ourselves to fit another
individual's lifestyle, nor are we asking them to change to
fit ours. We are simply learning how two individuals operate, how they interrelate and what kind of chemistry is
created between them.

Some people fit into our lives in a positive, enhancing
way and others seem to have exactly the opposite effect.
The point is, what are we learning from these interactions
and are they offering us the chance to grow as individuals? It is my hope to present techniques for the readers
of this book to help further analyze and understand their
own relationship needs and desires.

This book is about you, your likes, dislikes, needs, emotional considerations, physical and sexual drives. Basically, it explores what you seek to be happy in a relationship.

WHY ASTROLOGY?

Understanding planetary movement and cycles and knowing one's own astrological chart can bring great clarity and understanding. Astrology has many uses in today's world, but one of the best and most helpful for me has been to utilize it in regard to understanding the personal dynamics of an individual or the personal dynamics of two individuals interacting together. Compatibility studies through astrology seem to me to be an excellent way of observing behavior patterns, seeing problems and locating solutions to those problems.

The chart of the planets, signs and houses has been called a blueprint, a master plan, a mirror and even a photograph of the soul. It is completely faultless, error-free. It is perfection - like a perfectly tuned instrument. And like musicians, we seek a harmonious person/instrument/chart to play love's exquisite duet.

In September, 1974 I attended my very first astrology class in Glendale, California. One class led to another until my interest in astrology grew, expanded and finally consumed me. But the subject of astrology and the types of research that are open in the field are vast, and like most astrologers, I am still learning. When I obtained a copy of Rob Hand's <u>Planets In Composite</u> and began calculating composite charts, I became very excited about the potential there for indepth relationship analysis. The composite chart truly captures the essence of a couple's interaction. This led me to many composite calculations, data gathering and finally data sharing, and thus, this manuscript. In working with relationship astrology continuously in my practice, I have been unable to find a textbook that covers a broad scope of compatibility analysis in astrology. So, I decided to put down on paper the information I have gathered thus far. I hope people will find it useful as a general textbook/reference book for relationship astrology, and that beginners as well as professionals can benefit from the information contained herein.

Enjoy, and happy relationships!

CHAPTER 1

PLANETARY CYCLES
OF MARRIAGE AND DIVORCE

This chapter explores and celebrates the passage of all the planets of our solar system through the astrological sign of Libra during the 20th Century.

THE OUTER PLANETS THROUGH LIBRA

In 1942, Neptune led the way of the outer planets into Libra. Pluto finished its transit through Libra in August, 1984. In the 42 years between 1942 and 1984, every outer planet (Jupiter, Saturn, Chiron, Uranus, Neptune and Pluto) has moved through the sign Libra. During this 42-year period, the whole concept of marriage has changed drastically. Marriage is no longer "for better or worse, 'til death do us part," as it once was.

It is remarkable that in a 42 year period, all of the outer planets would transit any 30 degree segment of the zodiac. Of course, each year we see the inner planets (Sun, Moon, Mercury and Venus) transit through each sign of the zodiac in a relatively short period of time. The outer planets, however, spend much more time in a sign, return to each sign less frequently, and therefore impact the signs' principles more significantly. This historic passage of the outer planets through Libra signifies an important turning point for us as individuals, as couples and for all of humanity.

The domain of Libra is relationships - all one-to-one relationships including and especially marriage. During the passage of the planets through Libra, relationships have been challenged and changed.

To understand the discussion of relationships this book includes, it is important to understand the astrological sign Libra. Libra is the Latin word for balance and the zodiacal sign is symbolized by a set of scales. The major concern in Libra is how much of ourselves are we willing to

1

contribute to make other people our equals, our confidants, our mirror images. Libra questions, "Are the scales balanced? Are you giving as much as you're receiving in this partnership?" Each planet transiting Libra has made us examine this question, and has posed the question in a different tone – from the gentleness of Venus to the shocking revolution of Uranus.

The outer planets (sometimes called the generational planets) are of primary concern when examining the phenomenon of change in relationships during the last 42 years. Operating within each sign from one to 30 years, the generational planets shape the character of entire groups or generations of people. Table 1-1 capsulizes some of the issues confronted during the period between 1942 and 1984, and lists the years during that time when each of the outer planets visited Libra.

When Pluto entered Leo in the early 1940's, Neptune entered Libra, giving birth to what blossomed in the 1960's as the "flower generation." These postwar babies, having just observed the devastation of World War II, incarnated as a generation that would, en masse, make a statement against war. The slogan of the day, so appropriate for idealistic Neptune in the peace and love sign Libra, was "make love, not war." Interestingly enough, Libra is also the sign of open enemies that are confronted directly. The flower generation did not shy away from confrontation where its ideals mattered.

So how has the passage of all the planets through this partnership-oriented sign affected us? Significant changes have occurred in marriage and divorce laws, community property settlements and courtroom confrontations, all of which relate to the sign Libra. The once intimate partner has become an open enemy in the drama of the courtroom.

Sexual roles and role models have also changed drastically. There are two principles at work responsible for these changes. Sexual power comes under the sign Scorpio and its ruling planet Pluto. Pluto has been in Libra for the last 12 years, the sign concerned with one-to-one relationships. Women have made a statement to become liberated, and men are taking responsibility for issues which at one time did not concern them. Men are now looking into child rearing and domestic concerns as a viable alternative for career while women are comfortable working in construction, engineering and welding. Even transexual operations are being performed as never before. The choices are available now.

Some of the greatest reforms in interpersonal relationships took place during the 1960's. At that time, Uranus was entering the sign of Libra. Uranus is noted for shattering preconceived ideas and modes of behavior that have become out of date or no longer useful to society. It offers new concepts and ideas, but only if we let go of the old to make way for the new. Uranus' passage through Venus-ruled Libra brought a demand for equality for women and shattered the preconceived roles women once had in society. The women's movement was able to make its most successful

Table 1-1
Outer Planets' Movement Through Libra

PLANET	TOTAL CYCLE (YEARS)	TIME IN A SIGN (YEARS)	TIME IN LIBRA	MESSAGE OF PLANET THROUGH LIBRA
PLUTO	248	12 - 30	1972-1984	PLUTO TRANSFORMS. In Libra, the transformation process dealt with relationships in general and women (a Venus-ruled sign) more specifically.
NEPTUNE	165	14	1942-1957	NEPTUNE IDEALIZES AND IDOLIZES. In Libra, the message of Neptune gave birth to a generation of flower children seeking peace and love. Neptune's effect was to idealize relationships and idolize women. The Playboy bunny was born and the ultrasensual sex goddess of the screen was fantasized.
URANUS	84	7	1968-1974	URANUS AWAKENS/REBELS. In Libra, Uranus had the effect of awakening the masses to the need for women's lib (e.g., bra burning was popular). Both marriage and relationships began challenging old laws.
CHIRON	55	3-5	1944-1947	CHIRON SEARCHES FOR THE IDEAL. During Chiron's passage through Libra, which coincided with Jupiter and Neptune transits of Libra, marriage and divorce rates soared.
SATURN	29	2-3	1921-1924 1951-1953 1980-1983	SATURN TESTS/DISCIPLINES. Saturn has shared each of its passages through the sign of Libra with another planet which has maximized its effects. In 1921 and 1981, it joined Jupiter there; in 1952, it rendezvoused with Neptune; in 1982, it faced Pluto. Each period has resulted in a strengthening or testing of marriage, with more responsible affirmative actions for women.
JUPITER	12	1	see Fig 1-1	JUPITER EXPANDS. Since 1921, Jupiter has shared its spotlight in Libra with other planets which has magnified its effects. In Libra, Jupiter as a rule has the influence of making the marriage issue more important.

3

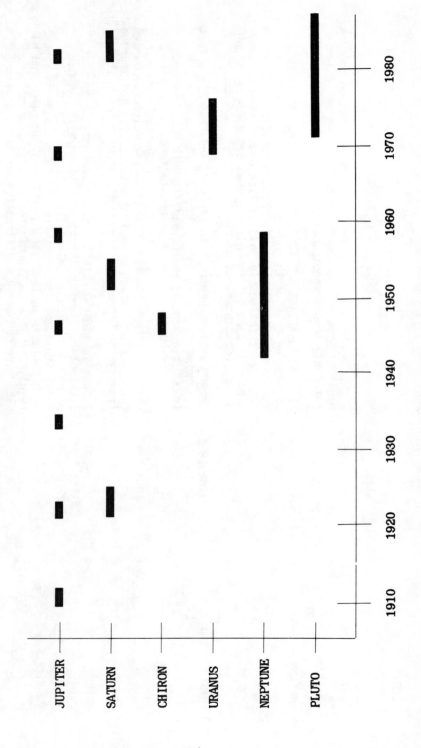

Figure 1-1
Outer Planet Transits of Libra, 1910–1985

4

strides during that time, with a little help from Uranus. In 1982, however, Libra hosted the somewhat hostile transit of Mars, Saturn and Pluto and the Equal Rights Amendment failed to pass.

These major transits through Libra have had a significant effect on women and their attitudes toward social/sexual roles and partnerships in general. Women are associated with Venus and its ruling sign Libra, and women have had massive reawakenings, transformations and new responsibilities to deal with as a result of the passage of these planets through Libra.

The 20th Century has brought women to a unique time in terms of their own evolution and growth, both individually and collectively. Prior to the 1940's when the first outer planet entered Libra in this century, marriages were fairly stable. Marriages were on the upswing and divorces were few and far between. There did not exist a need to keep marriages "growing" on a transformational and transpersonal level as there does in the 1980's. Role models for marriage partners were fairly simple and there was no need to exceed those boundaries. Since the passage of all the outer planets through the marriage sign Libra, however, there has been and continues to be a growing need among people everywhere to seek awareness, fine tuning, transformation and transpersonal growth among themselves and their partners. People are seeking to look at themselves (Aries) through their relationships (polarity Libra). In the days before the transformational planets entered Libra, self growth (Aries) was often sacrificed for the good of the marriage (Libra). Today, that has reversed. Many marriages are sacrificed for the sake of personal growth.

In the 1940's and 1950's, Woman was an idealized goddess (Neptune through Libra) conceived on the screen and acted out in love. She moved herself and her family to the suburbs and was so busy liberating herself of physical hardships with the addition of blenders, electric can openers, no-wax floors, and washers and dryers, she had very little time or energy left for intellectual and/or spiritual growth. She was Cinderella who had been whisked away to the suburbs by Prince Charming. She was not supposed to think. All she had to do was operate the appliances and make herself, her house and her children look beautiful in this fairy tale that was supposed to have a happy ending. It was up to her husband to worry about the mortgage, the car loan and the doctor bills.

Uranus' seven year passage through a sign makes the most dramatic statements of any of the planets about the principles of that sign, as that is Uranus' function. When Uranus entered Libra in the 1960's, women began thinking of reform and awakening. They were no longer satisfied with the Cinderella story. They no longer believed the fairy tale, and they united to make a dramatic statement. They tossed their bras into the fire as their symbolic gesture of sending their 1950's Playboy bunny image up in smoke. They wanted freedom intellectually. They wanted freedom in the workplace. They demanded equality.

5

By 1972 when Pluto entered Libra, women began a strong period of transformation as they attempted to find themselves, their own purpose and their own power (Pluto). They sought to understand their sexual identity as well. No longer satisfied with being the sexual object, many women decided to turn the tables and become the sexual predator.

The early 1980's have brought the culmination of this rebirth (still Pluto, with an added emphasis of a Jupiter/Saturn conjunction in 1981 and a Pluto/Saturn conjunction in 1982-83 in Libra). The result has been and will be new forms of responsibility, duty, initiative and increased sexual power for women.

The woman of the 1980's has been injected with a substantial dosage of yang energy. She has accepted the challenge (for the most part) of switching the sexual role when circumstances dictate that she do so, and does quite well at managing, organizing and planning executive moves, while alternately baking cookies, bearing children and doing laundry. With Pluto activating Libra, she has become sexually liberated and awakened, enjoying and even seeking out the opportunity to be the sexually aggressive partner. Her desires are more intense; she is highly stimulated and charged.

This process has been rough, however, for many women and men have not accepted these new roles. Many men are uncomfortable with women's increased sexual and social needs and desires. The male ego in many cases still requires he be in charge of these affairs, and he is somewhat turned off by woman's sudden aggressiveness, resulting in much sexual and social conflict. Since man is unable to respond quickly to these needs, woman is not fully satisfied. Many men are also threatened by woman's increased strength, domination and achievement in the business and professional world, a world which has traditionally been man's domain.

This, of course, is not true for all men. There are thousands of men and women who are working very hard at breaking stereotyped sexual patterns that have been around for centuries. But because these patterns have been around for centuries, it is more than just you and I working on accepting the concept of equality in relationships; it is the entire collective unconscious of man and woman who are involved in creating new models. New role models are threatening to most people because the security of what they've had or how they've acted in the past is gone. The new role model is uncharted territory and often requires stumbling in the dark until it has been refined.

The message the generational planets passing through Libra in the 1980's has brought to relationships and to women is that the role models may be exchanged and may be shared by the partners. If the man is no longer to be the dominant partner to the woman's submissive role, then neither will the reverse be true. The Equal Rights Amendment will not pass nor will the women's movement grasp the foothold it is trying to secure until the voice of woman is united in efforts of cooperation and sharing. Wars are not won by creating more strife and hostility, but by sitting at the peace table, mediating, negotiating, possibly giving something up, but also getting something in return. "Man" is not the enemy, but the polarity through which harmony and balance may be achieved.

What about personal relationships, then? Basically, many men still look for women who will mother them. They look for the idealized 1950's woman: soft, sensual, ultra-feminine and passive. Though most women can be that woman some of the time, many are no longer content to be that woman all of the time - not since the transformation.

Instead of making the effort to understand this sudden power and domination, he turns away, at times towards other men - hence the sudden surge of male homosexuality. However, only a small percentage have taken that route. The majority, not knowing how to deal with the problem, silently withdraw and become passive-resistant or look for new partnerships, only to be confronted by the same dilemma.

Although increasingly more men are awakening, the majority are still living in the past regarding sexual and social liberation. We are, after all, in the infancy of this role reversal and revolution. For millennia, women have been yin - the passive, receptive force, created to bear children and provide nurturing for the family. Changes of this nature are not made overnight and not without suffering.

Time, however, will effect these changes. By the time Saturn makes its next entry into Libra (early 21st Century), the balance will have been achieved. An entire generation or more will have grown up and experienced Mom in the job market and Dad fixing dinner. Men will understand and experience the everyday flexibility with which one can integrate yin and yang. Meanwhile, only through individual effort on the part of all will couples achieve that important balance for which they are striving.

In the late 1980's, equality in relationships will not be a major issue because the extremes have already been expressed. Pluto took its last steps through Libra in August, 1984, thus completing the transformational identity of relationships. The 14 years Pluto spends in Scorpio from 1984 to 1996 will affect relationships on a different level. Libra's message was equality in relationships, including cooperation, sharing and interfacing. Scorpio's message is about sharing on a more interpersonal level - the sharing of resources and of power drives. But before we can settle into the comfortable routine of marriage and family life, we had to witness extremes of thought and life-style. This was so a choice could be offered to those who are still willing to postpone marriage or childbearing or who choose to eliminate marriage altogether from their lives in order to seek fulfillment in new and unexplored social, professional, sexual and ideological roles.

These two planets add focus and dimension in short-range terms to the signs through which they are passing. Mars is said to fall in Libra, while Venus is said to be dignified by its rulership of Libra. Because these transits last for such a short time, it is impossible to make any evaluations as to their effects upon the masses regarding relationships and marriage. However, observing their forward and retrograde movements along with their conjunction/opposition periods is guaranteed to bring you valid results when checked against your personal chart and love/marriage life. The observations of Mars/Venus retrogrades is particularly important to these issues because they are the archetypal planetary pair for love and romance. Additionally, noting the years Mars and Venus make their conjunction and opposition to one another adds importance to the general tone of love and marriage issues.

Retrograde (Rx) is a phenomenon whereby a planet appears to move backwards through the zodiac as viewed from planet Earth. Retrograde is nothing more than another astrological statement that suggests some sort of reversal in a planet's energy or behavior pattern. Because astrology is a symbolic language to begin with, we must observe all of its patterns and translate them into facts. People are often quite unaware of what is motivating them when planets are retrograde because the effects seem to manifest on an unconscious level for the masses. People sense that something different is occurring and they begin to question values and reassess relationship needs. My personal observation is that when Mars (a yang, masculine planetary energy that rules Aries) turns retrograde, issues are brought up by men who are looking within and evaluating personal issues that may not be satisfactory in their relationships. When Mars is retrograde, self assertion, competition, sexual compatibility and anger all need redefinition. Mars retrograde periods may be interpreted as internalization and redefinition of those energies.

When Venus is retrograde, women seem to be the ones who are analyzing, reviewing and pulling back. For instance, if Venus turns retrograde in Cancer, a woman might analyze her position in the home, her position as mother and issues regarding emotional security. The period when Venus is retograde tests marriages and relationships in such areas as equality, sharing and cooperation.

Tables 1-2 and 1-3 show the years and the signs in which Mars and Venus turned stationary/retrograde (SRx) between 1940 and 1999. Only twice during this 60-year period did their retrograde cycles overlap - for a few days in February, 1950 and again for a few days in May, 1969. Of 37 Venus stationary retrogrades in this period, eight of them occurred in the sign Virgo and seven in Cancer. This sum constitutes 41% of the total retrogrades of Venus. Can we interpret this as a statement for this period of history concerning the role of women in the home (Cancer) and in the workplace (Virgo)? Additionally, Venus retrograded

Table 1-2
Mars and Venus Stationary Retrograde, 1940-1969

YEAR	♈	♉	♊	♋	♌	♍	♎	♏	♐	♑	♒	♓
1940				♀								
1941	♂											
1942											♀	
1943			♂			♀						
1944												
1945		♀			♂							
1946									♀			
1947												
1948				♀		♂						
1949												
1950							♂				♀	
1951						♀						
1952								♂				
1953		♀										
1954								♀		♂		
1955												
1956				♀								♂
1957												
1958			♂								♀	
1959						♀						
1960				♂								
1961	♀											
1962				♂				♀				
1963												
1964				♀								
1965						♂						
1966											♀	
1967						♀		♂				
1968												
1969	♀								♂			

Table 1-3
Mars and Venus Stationary Retrograde, 1970–1999

YEAR	♈	♉	♊	♋	♌	♍	♎	♏	♐	♑	♒	♓
1970								♀				
1971											♂	
1972				♀								
1973		♂										
1974											♀	
1975				♂		♀						
1976												
1977	♀				♂							
1978								♀				
1979												
1980				♀		♂						
1981												
1982							♂					
1983						♀						
1984								♂				
1985	♀											
1986								♀		♂		
1987												
1988	♂			♀								
1989												
1990			♂								♀	
1991						♀						
1992				♂								
1993	♀											
1994								♀				
1995						♂						
1996			♀									
1997							♂				♀	
1998												
1999						♀		♂				

seven times in Aquarius, six times in Scorpio and five times in Aries, highly independent, self motivated signs. This highly uneven distribution of Venus SRx through the signs suggests certain themes to be dominant in relationship issues for this period. Venus avoided turning retrograde in Libra, Capricorn and Pisces during this period.

Mars makes an entirely different statement in its retrogrades for this period. Of the 28 times it retrograded during this cycle, four occurred in Scorpio, four in Virgo and three in Leo. Two of these signs, Leo and Scorpio, deal prominently with sexual issues. Highly publicized issues of the times have dealt with sexual role models, an increasingly high percentage of male homosexuality and sexual role reversals. Mars has left no sign untouched in its retrograde stations, covering each sign at least once.

A look at Tables 1-2 and 1-3 to elicit personal information concerning love, romance, marriage and divorce may be helpful. When Venus retrogrades over an important point in your chart (Sun, Moon, angles, etc.), you may see a direct reversal in marital status. In other words, if married, it may signal a separation (even if temporary) or call attention to strains in the relationship; if single, it may indicate an important love affair or marriage. Remember, the retrograde cycle offers three chances to contact a point in your chart, not just one. Important issues are in the works and are being stated during a planet's retrograde cycle over a point in your chart. Generally, however, Venus does bring the coming together of love, sharing and cooperation in some form.

Marriage and Divorce Statistics for the United States

When choosing to embark upon a study of marriage and divorce as related to the planetary cycles, what was obvious to me was that marriage and divorce customs, preferences and laws have changed drastically in the United States since the end of World War II. Marriages seemed much more stable and enduring, whereas divorces were few and far between during the early part of the 20th Century. Today that trend has reversed. Divorce is as common as marriage in many parts of the country, and multiple marriage is more popular than the "'til death do us part" liaison.

As mentioned earlier, during the period 1942-1984 all of the outer planets have transited through Libra, the sign that traditionally governs marriage and divorce in astrology. Figure 1-1 shows the years that each of the outer planets occupied Libra in the tropical zodiac from 1910 to 1979.

Figure 1-2, which shows the total number of marriages and divorces in the United States during these 70 years, reveals some startling facts. In 1910, there were 930,000 marriages and 80,000 divorces or about 11.5 times as many

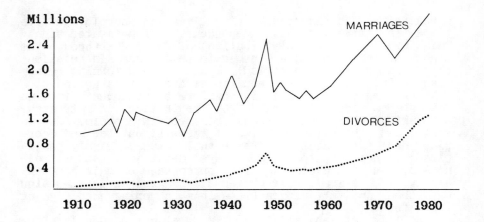

Figure 1-2
Total Number of Marriages and Divorces
in the United States, 1910-1979

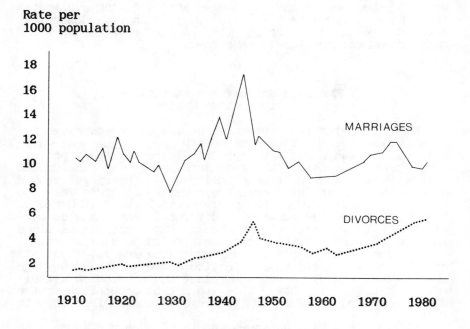

Figure 1-3
Marriage and Divorce rates
in the United States, 1910-1979

marriages as divorces. By 1979, these numbers had changed
dramatically. While the total number of marriages had increased by a factor of 2.5 to 2,350,000, divorces increased
by a factor of almost 15, to 1,170,000. In other words, in
1979, there were only twice as many marriages as there were
divorces. Figure 1-2 shows that the number of divorces
increased most dramatically from the mid-1960s to 1979.
Another period to note is 1940-1950 when there was a sharp
increase in divorces, culminating in 1946, followed by a
sharp decrease.

Marriage and divorce rates between 1910 and 1979, which
are depicted graphically in Figure 1-3, show similar trends
and reinforce what has been described previously. In 1910,
there were 10.3 marriages and 0.9 divorces per thousand
population. By 1979, people were getting married at a rate
of 10.7 marriages per thousand population, almost no change
from the marriage rate of 1910. However by 1979, the divorce rate had increased to 5.3 per thousand population, a
factor of almost six greater than the divorce rate in 1910.

While the marriage rate has fluctuated considerably
since 1910 (particularly from 1930 to 1950), no clear long-
term trend is evident, and today the same percentage of
people are getting married as there were in 1910. However,
divorce rates on the average have steadily increased with
time. The most dramatic periods of change in the divorce
rate were from 1940 to 1950 and 1965 to 1979. Table 1-4
lists the average marriage and divorce rates for each of
the ten year periods between 1910 and 1979. A look at the
data shows further reinforcement for what is being said
here.

Table 1-4
Average 10 year Marriage and Divorce Rates
in the United States, 1910-1979

10-YEAR PERIOD	AVERAGE MARRIAGE RATE (per thousand)	AVERAGE DIVORCE RATE (per thousand)
1910-19	10.4	1.1
1920-29	10.5	1.6
1930-39	9.8	1.7
1940-49	12.5	2.9
1950-59	9.5	2.4
1960-69	9.3	2.5
1970-79	10.5	4.6

When Figures 1-2 and 1-3 are compared to Figure 1-1, some interesting facts are revealed. The two time periods which showed the greatest changes in either divorces and/or marriages also coincide with major outer planet transits through the sign Libra. The period from 1940 to 1950 saw sharp increases in both marriages and divorces. Both peaked in 1946, which coincided with the end of World War II, a time when three of the outer planets (Jupiter, Chiron and Neptune) were transiting Libra. In addition, there was a Venus/Mars conjunction in the sign of Libra in August, 1946.

Following 1946, there was a sharp drop in both marriages and divorces, both of which leveled off somewhat until the mid-1960's, when both began a steady rise. In 1968, Uranus entered Libra and the entire seven year passage of Uranus through Libra showed divorce on a relatively rapid climb, surpassing its previous 1946 peak.

In 1971 Pluto entered Libra and divorce continued its dramatic rise through 1979. Pluto finished its transit of Libra in August, 1984. Unfortunately, marriage and divorce data were not available beyond 1979 at the time of this writing, but the trends appear clear. Perhaps the outer planets have shaken the roots of Libra by their passage through this sign such that now marriages and divorces take place at about the same frequency.

Chapter 2

COMPONENTS OF
THE ASTROLOGICAL CHART

What happens in the first few minutes that we meet someone? Do we immediately tune into that person as if he/she
were a long lost friend or lover? Do we feel an electric
charge that says, "That person rubs me the wrong way," and
run the other way? Or do we spend the remainder of the
meeting analyzing, evaluating and judging that person? A
person's manner, color and style of dress, his or her physical build and body language, and the amount of eye contact
that is made all contribute to that initial determination
of compatibility. What is said also has a major impact, as
Leonard Zunin in his book, Contact: The First Four Minutes
(1981), suggests:

"What two people communicate during their first four
minutes of contact is so crucial that it will determine
whether strangers will remain strangers or will become
acquaintances, friends, lovers or lifetime mates."

Later, as we get to know more about the other person
through verbal exchange and shared activities, we accept
those parts that we relate to and reject those parts that
we do not comprehend or for which we are unwilling to make
adjustments. It is not necessary to accept each person we
relate to 100 percent. We are all unique and individual,
but our instinctive longing to be accepted by other
individuals causes us to make adjustments and compensations
for a moment in order to relate to others. It is here that
we can look to the astrological chart as a frame of
reference for who we are, what we are looking for in a mate
and how that mate fits our mold.
To be able to understand how two charts fit together,
we must first look at the components of a single chart and
determine its message. That brings us to the first step -
the 12 astrological signs.

15

THE 12 SIGNS

The 12 signs of the zodiac are the most widely known and most frequently discussed part of astrology. Almost everyone knows their sign, that is, the sign in which the Sun was placed on the day of their birth. The sun signs contribute to the psychological attitudes and make-up of an individual, yet it is the sequence of the 12 signs that give color and meaning to a chart. You are different from every other person of your sun sign because of the unique placement of your signs and planets around the wheel of the horoscope and their interaction with each other.

Although signs follow a sequence that never changes, the wheel of time turns. While Aries may be the first house at 6:00 a.m. on March 21st, it will be the 7th house at 6:00 p.m. on the same day. Thus, the time you were born makes your wheel unique.

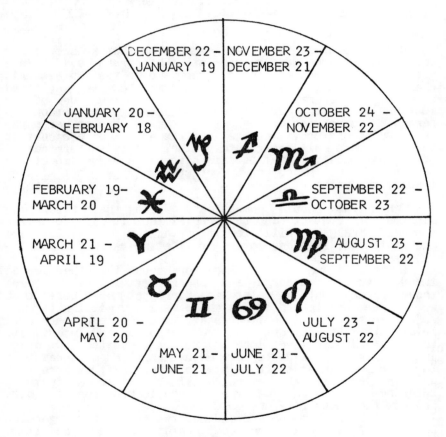

Figure 2-1
Signs: The 365 Day Year

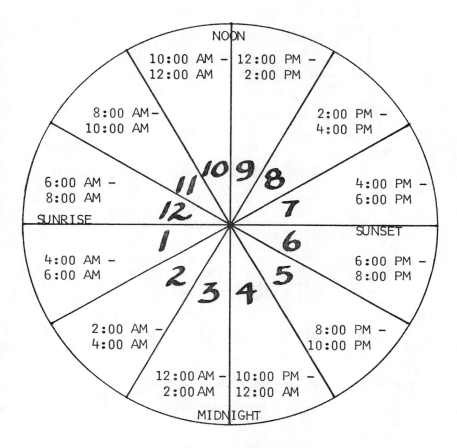

Figure 2-2
Houses: The 24 Hour Day

Figure   2-1   illustrates   the   days   of the year the Sun
passes   through   each   sign of the zodiac, thus representing
our   calendar   year.   Figure   2-1   illustrates   how   the
horoscopic   wheel   is   also   representative   of   the 24-hour
clock,   showing   the hours of the day the Sun passes through
each house of the zodiac.
        The   12   signs   in sequence are contained in every horo-
scope.   What gives a sign expression is the number and character   of   planets in that sign.   A sign would be considered
active   if   one   or more planets are placed in it.   The more
planets   placed   in one sign, the more obvious and sometimes
exaggerated the behavior becomes.
        I   use the following list of planets and points within a
chart   to   determine   the emphasis of each sign in the horoscope.

17

Sun	Uranus
Moon	Neptune
Mercury	Pluto
Venus	North Node
Mars	South Node
Jupiter	Ascendant
Saturn	Midheaven

# of Points per sign in a chart	Degree of expression
0	EXTREME. The expression of the sign's energy is either non-existent because of the lack of points or extremely strong to overcompensate for the lack of points.
1-2	AVERAGE. There would usually be a normal expression of the sign's energy. One or two planets per sign is one of the most common placements.
3-4	STRONG. There is usually a heavy expression of the principles of this sign in one's behavior patterns.
5 or more	EXTREME. Here we find a highly focused and often rigid personality structure (ego) seeking constant outlet for energy.

Figure 2-3, the Horoscope of Mick Jagger, illustrates what we would label as "extreme," with 5 planets plus the Ascendant expressing themselves through the sign Leo.

It is not easy to give sign interpretations without running the risk of generalizing. Astrologers stress the interaction of the 12 signs in sequence, along with the planetary activity within each sign, so that the chart may be viewed as a whole rather than as a fragment. Interpreting becomes an exact art only when dealing with the entire wheel.

Yet, there must be a place to start with guidelines to follow when analyzing the sign meanings. Because we are dealing with relationship analysis, the following interpretations are geared toward understanding how each sign and planet approaches relationships.

Terms used for the signs are well aspected and stressful. This does not necessarily mean that stressful refers to a square and well aspected refers to a trine. The level of integration one has reached within oneself and how one

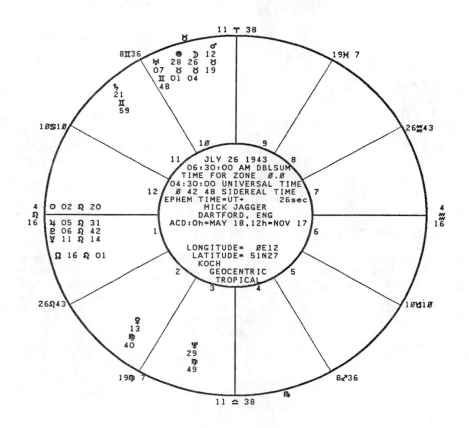

Figure 2-3
Horoscope of Mick Jagger

handles or expresses one's chart would be a more accurate
representation for these terms. We always have the choice
to handle the energies any way we choose; sometimes that
comes out "stressfully" and other times that comes out
"well executed or aspected."

ARIES

"I'm running down the road trying to loosen my load
I've got seven women on my mind.
Four that wanna own me, two that wanna stone me,
One says she's a friend of mine..."

Jackson Browne & Glenn Frey
"Take It Easy"

ELEMENT: FIRE
QUALITY: CARDINAL
PLANET: MARS
HOUSE: 1 (PERSONAL IDENTITY)

NATURE: (+) energetic, shows initiative and drive, restlessness, leadership ability, youthful, playful, assertive
(-) self-centered, lacks follow through, hot headed, impatient, impulsive

WELL ASPECTED PLANETS IN ARIES:

The Aries individual easily and comfortably initiates relationships in all kinds of social settings. Aries is Mars ruled and is physically active. There is usually high sex drive, and passions are expressed frequently. The cardinal nature of Aries produces someone who is able to act on little notice when motivated to go out and get something. The fire nature suggests a lively spirit. They can usually get away with outrageous behavior due to a child-like innocence they exhibit as part of their impulsive nature. Discovery of the self is their goal, therefore their actions are considered self-centered by others. Aries usually is motivated to act on impulse and needs no approval or recognition from others for such actions.

STRESSFUL ASPECTS TO PLANETS IN ARIES:

Aries' negative side is selfishness. Libra, which is Aries' polar opposite and through which Aries is learning to operate, stresses compromise and cooperation with the partner. Therefore, Aries must learn to give in a relationship. They must learn to think of their partner more than just occasionally instead of always thinking in terms of "me first." Often Aries is the outgoing, sociable one and the partner is the quiet, more reflective one. Heavily stressed placements in Aries can produce childish outbursts of anger or "temper tantrums," depicting an emotionally immature individual.

TAURUS

"I get a peaceful, easy feeling
And I know you won't let me down,
'Cause I'm already standing on the   ground..."

Jack Tempchin
"Peaceful Easy Feeling"

ELEMENT:	EARTH
QUALITY:	FIXED
PLANET:	VENUS OR BACCHUS (TRANSPLUTO)
HOUSE:	2 (RESOURCE$, VALUES)

NATURE: (+) solid, stable, patient, enduring,
thoughtful, resourceful, musical, artistic
(-) lazy, procrastinator, materialistically
driven, possessive, stubborn, insecure

WELL ASPECTED PLANETS IN TAURUS:

The fixed nature of this sign suggests a concern for
establishing security, one of building and consolidating on
the material plane throughout their life. The earth of
Taurus enjoys and needs creature comforts, a relaxed, earthy atmosphere and fine food, music and the arts. A highly
physical and sensual interaction may develop when Taurus is
dominant. Relationships will focus on these elements,
along with a need to view self-worth through those things
the Taurus possesses. Because it is a fixed sign, it is
concerned with collecting and gathering, usually indicating
a surplus or abundance.

STRESSFUL ASPECTS TO PLANETS IN TAURUS:

Stressful planets in Taurus often create an attitude
that "the world owes me a living." They have to constantly
balance their strong desire nature (polarity Scorpio) and
realize the material rewards they expect from life are in
direct proportion to the efforts they put forth to make
them a reality. Possessiveness and jealousy have to be
worked out when there are stressful aspects in Taurus. One
partner may expect more than the other is willing to give.
Horns may lock in argument because neither partner will
yield nor concede to the other. Arguments often center
around money (or lack of it) as well as values. What they
earn and how they spend their earnings can be a major challenge for the stressed Taurus and a major topic of conversation with their partner.

GEMINI

"I've looked at love from both sides now
From up and down, and still somehow,
It's love's illusions I recall
I really don't know love at all..."

Joni Mitchell
"Both Sides Now"

ELEMENT: AIR
QUALITY: MUTABLE
PLANET: MERCURY
HOUSE: 3 (COMMUNICATIONS, CONSCIOUS MIND)

NATURE: (+) intellectual, curious, quick-witted,
              communicative, stimulating, multitalented
              (-) dualistic, restless, nervous, flighty,
              scattered, superficial, repetitive

WELL-ASPECTED PLANETS IN GEMINI:

Gemini is a talkative and playful individual who may
seek to share a similar thought process with their partner.
They would likely be one whose goals center on education,
teaching, talking, writing or working with their hands. An
overriding need for Gemini, being of the air element, is
communicating clearly. In other words, they desire more
than anything else someone with whom they can truly feel
stimulated on a mental and verbal plane. Adaptability is
one of their finer points (being a mutable sign) with not
only a curiosity about other customs and life-styles, but a
willingness and ability to be whatever the situation calls
for at any given time.

STRESSFUL ASPECTS TO PLANETS IN GEMINI:

Gemini's ability to go off in six different directions
and end up nowhere but exhausted is one of their major
blocks in producing anything tangible. The thing that
drives most of their mates crazy is their ability to talk,
talk, talk about all their great ideas and produce few, if
any, tangible results. The tendency for them to become
bored easily can result in few solid, long-lasting relationships and many short-lived, somewhat shallow involvements.
Even those who do stay with one mate will find they
constantly need new stimulation where both parties are
learning and growing. Gemini, an air sign, will tend to
intellectualize feelings. They often turn off to outer
stimuli as a defense mechanism, so words just bounce off
and they may not hear what is being transmitted. When
stressfulness is felt through Gemini, the mind can become
so cluttered with trivia that resulting communication
becomes a problem. Through their polarity Sagittarius,

which represents the higher mind, they are learning to listen and learn instead of always being concerned with the transmission of information.

CANCER

"Tonight you're mine completely
You give your love so sweetly
Tonight the light of love is in your eyes,
But will you love me tomorrow..."

                                Carole King
                                "Will You Love Me Tomorrow"

ELEMENT:	WATER
QUALITY:	CARDINAL
PLANET:	MOON
HOUSE:	4 (HOME, EMOTIONAL SECURITY)
NATURE:	(+) sensitive, nurturing, receptive, intuitive, parental, protective
	(-) moody, defensive, easily hurt, insecure, possessive, worrisome

WELL-ASPECTED PLANETS IN CANCER:

Cancers immediately and automatically understand the needs, fears and motivations of others. They will usually try to protect another unless there is reason to feel threatened by or mistrustful of that person or situation. After all, self-preservation instincts are stronger in the crab than in any other sign. The cardinal and water combination is expressed by motivating and initiating feeling relationships with others. The watery nature of the sign, however, is so sensitive that Cancers will often put up a screen to protect themselves and withdraw into their shells for comfort and security.

STRESSFUL ASPECTS TO PLANETS IN CANCER:

Stressful activity in this sign often results in extreme moodiness, self-defensiveness and complaining. The need for love and affection is so strong in the insecure Cancer, it can sometimes be viewed as compulsive. Because Cancer worries about emotional security, the partner, no matter how much he or she does, never satisfies Cancer. Through its Capricorn polarity, Cancer is learning the meaning and nature of structure, form and responsibility. Where Capricorn can be somewhat restrained in its emotional expression, Cancers demonstrate "smother love." Moodiness is the number one issue Cancers' mate must learn to endure.

LEO

"Light of the world,
Shine on me,
Love is the answer..."

Todd Rungren
"Love is the Answer"

ELEMENT:	FIRE
QUALITY:	FIXED
PLANET:	SUN
HOUSE:	5 (SELF EXPRESSION AND WILL)
NATURE:	(+) proud, generous, creative, strong, warm, friendly, active, protective, expressive
	(-) overpowering, egocentric, melodramatic snobbish, needs much attention, flamboyant, unyielding

WELL-ASPECTED PLANETS IN LEO:

Leo combines love of life and spirit (fire) with the steadiness and consistency of the fixed signs. Leo, governing the heart, is love in its purest form. Leo expresses warmth, affection and love in a playful, often child-like manner. Strong on affection, Leo sees romance as an art form. Social activities and hobbies may dominate their attention as will theater, films or sports. Quite protective of self and offspring, the Leo's life revolves around strong relationships with those close to them. Their ability to offer humor and self-confidence is a welcome cure when others need a lift.

STRESSFUL ASPECTS TO PLANETS IN LEO:

Leo, governing the ego, can develop strong needs in this area when feeling insecure, and often needs center stage just to be happy. Leo's tendency to over-dramatize every situation can result in many inventive ploys to get attention whenever possible. Because they feel starved for affection, the stressed Leo often plays out the "naughty child" role, assuming any response is better than none. Leo works its polarity through Aquarius, a detached air sign, pursuing universal love, and is learning to balance that aspect with its strong emphasis on personal love. Caught between the polarities, Leo sometimes is more concerned with receiving than giving love. They are learning how to give love in its purest form, without thought of what they will receive in return.

24

VIRGO

"You can take me to paradise
And then again, you can be cold as ice.
I'm over my head
But it sure feels nice..."

Christine McVie
"Over My Head"

ELEMENT:	EARTH
QUALITY:	MUTABLE
PLANET:	MERCURY
HOUSE:	6 (SERVICE, WORK, HEALTH)

NATURE: (+) service-oriented, analytical, devoted, intelligent, efficient, organized, precise, dedicated
(-) critical, judgmental, sloppy, skeptical, hypochondriacal, pessimistic

WELL-ASPECTED PLANETS IN VIRGO:

Virgo represents the integration of the left and the right brains: intelligence and logic blended with sensitivity and compassion. Virgo's mutability adapts to any given situation. The earth grounds the physical into well thought-out, careful attention to the details at hand. They are dedicated to whatever or whomever comes their way at any given time, not particularly fond of more than one relationship at a time. While they are not always big on romance, they are devoted care-givers who offer their services lovingly to their mates. They will strive for intelligence and order in a relationship and often desire a mate with whom they can mentally and spiritually connect or one whose work is in the same field.

STRESSFUL ASPECTS TO PLANETS IN VIRGO:

The number one complaint of Virgo's mates is their workaholic addiction, which often leaves their mates feeling left out in the cold or unloved. Mercury's rulership of Virgo, like Gemini, is mentally inclined, but unlike Gemini who desires a variety of mental stimuli, Virgo tends to short-circuit when put on overload. Thus, Virgo's downfall when stressed can be an inability to handle too many problems at once. If the relationship and job both need attention simultaneously, one will virtually be ignored until the other is settled. Unfortunately for Virgo's mate, it is often the relationship that gets ignored. Critical judgment is w..ere Virgos hurt themselves. They over-analyze every move their partner makes, then inflict self blame. Prone to seeking perfection in form, Virgo works through its polarity Pisces, who desires perfection in the formless

(God and the universe). When stressed, Virgo finds countless imperfections and can complain about everything in
sight.

LIBRA

"Just the two of us
We can make it if we try
Just the two of us,
You and I..."

MacDonald, Salter & Withers
"Just the Two of Us"

ELEMENT:	AIR
QUALITY:	CARDINAL
PLANET:	VENUS
HOUSE:	7 (PARTNERSHIPS)
NATURE:	(+) fair, peaceful, cooperative, logical sociable, people-oriented, aesthetic
	(-) lazy, non-committal, unmotivated, vain, judgmental, indecisive

WELL-ASPECTED PLANETS IN LIBRA:

The merging of cardinality (initiative) and air (social
relationships) results in Libra's position on the wheel as
the sign of partnerships, where we initiate social relations with others. Libra seeks a partner in life and will
often put relationship needs high above anything else. The
airiness of this Venus-ruled sign usually makes beauty,
love and harmony strong themes within the Libra's environment. Their charming, relaxed, laid-back nature is usually
comforting to most people.

STRESSFUL ASPECTS TO PLANETS IN LIBRA:

Libra, symbolized by the scales, can tip either end in
relationships when stressed. Libras may identify so much
with the partner that they may lose self-esteem or individuality. People pleasing, trying to make the other appreciate them and keeping the peace at any price are traits
which often keep Libras from truly exploring themselves
through their polarity, Aries. At the other end of the
scale, however, Libra may assume that once the relationship
has been cemented, there is no further need to develop it,
forcing the mate to be responsible for continued growth in
the relationship. Libras' love of "love" can prevent them
from really feeling love until it might be too late.

SCORPIO

"You can't always get what you want, Honey
You can't always get what you want,
But if you try sometime, yeah, you just might find
You get what you need!..."

Mick Jagger & Keith Richards
"You Can't Always Get What You
Want"

ELEMENT: WATER
QUALITY: FIXED
PLANET: PLUTO
HOUSE: 8 (PERSONAL TRANSFORMATION)

NATURE: (+) shrewd, probing, regenerative, sensual,
                mysterious, strong, scientific, psychic
                (-) possessive, revengeful, vindictive,
                temperamental, extremes of mood, suspicious,
                jealous

WELL-ASPECTED PLANETS IN SCORPIO:

In Scorpio, the water (feeling) element combines with
the fixed mode to create deeply held feelings. As a rule,
Scorpio does not like casual relationships. They desire
relationships that will strike a chord to the depth of
their beings. Scorpio seeks transformation, and their deeply felt relationships will always bring them personal renew-
al in one sense or another. They are looking for the soulmate, preferring all or nothing at all in a relationship.
They are protective of those they love and seek to strength-
en the bonds between them so they might both transcend the
nature of physical love. Healing is one of the gifts they
bring to a relationship, along with the ability to break
down all the walls, layers and masks that exist around
their partner in order to penetrate and bring to the surface the most deeply buried layers of feeling and emotion.

STRESSFUL ASPECTS TO PLANETS IN SCORPIO:

As with Scorpio's polarity, Taurus, the testing ground
can come with holding, possessing or manipulating those
close to them. With Taurus, the possessions are usually
things, but with Scorpio, the possessions are generally
people. In any case, they are both signs that need to work
through jealousy and possessiveness in relationships.
There is a strong need in Scorpio, especially when stressful placements occur, to control and dominate relationships. This is usually done through Scorpio's tools, money
and/or sex. Their obsessions and strong needs can drive
relationships from their lives. Being a water sign, they

cling to feelings, and it is hard for them to let go of
pain and hurt from the past. Because of this, they often
carefully guard their past or secrets, allowing few, if
any, to penetrate their deep core.

SAGITTARIUS

"You're a rambler and a gambler
And a sweet talking ladies' man
And you love your lovin'
But not like you love your freedom..."

Joni Mitchell
"Help Me"

ELEMENT:	FIRE
QUALITY:	MUTABLE
PLANET:	JUPITER
HOUSE:	9 (PHILOSOPHY, HIGHER MIND)
NATURE:	(+) outgoing, broad-minded, knowledgeable, philosophical, goal-oriented, freedom loving, visionary
	(−) know-it-all, pretentious, judgmental, hypocritical, voracious, vain, opinionated, blunt, unreliable

WELL-ASPECTED PLANETS IN SAGITTARIUS:

The Sagittarius individual expresses his fiery zest for
life and learning through mutability: the desire for an
ever-changing arena of personal expression. Exploring new
avenues and reaching vistas never before attempted are well
within Sagittarius's grasp. In partnerships, they seek the
role of student and teacher, judge and philosopher. They
seek a partner with whom they can live, laugh, love and
learn. The restless nature of this sign also involves giving their partner room to breathe, to explore on their own
so they may grow as individuals, thus contributing much
more to the relationship. Sagittarius is one who seeks the
best life has to offer.

STRESSFUL ASPECTS TO PLANETS IN SAGITTARIUS:

The stressed out Sagittarius has a terrible time accepting anythng that would stifle their freedom to move and
explore. If forced into a meager lifestyle or commonplace,
routine existence, they are like caged animals. Stressful
planetary placements in Sagittarius can result in them living way beyond their means, becoming victims of a debt-
ridden, credit card-infected society. The Sagittarians'

zealousness for candid speech (bluntness) without fore-thought often results in poor timing or a partner's hurt feelings. The polarity of Gemini helps to ground the infor-mation and give it practical application. When stressed, Sagittarius, like the other fire signs, runs the risk of being the selfish one, not considering their partner's feel-ings or desires. They have the tendency to take off in search of greener pastures rather than staying and attemp-ting to work out the problems confronting them.

CAPRICORN

"Will you still need me
Will you still feed me
When I'm sixty-four..."

John Lennon & Paul McCartney
"When I'm Sixty-Four"

ELEMENT: EARTH
QUALITY: CARDINAL
PLANET: SATURN
HOUSE: 10 (SOCIETY, PROFESSION)

NATURE: (+) responsible, organized, ambitious,
                cautious, prudent, realistic, aloof
                (-) worrisome, depressive, restrictive,
                fearful, easily threatened, suspicious

WELL-ASPECTED PLANETS IN CAPRICORN:

Capricorn is a cardinal earth sign, expressing initia-tive and useful actions that create productive substance on the physical (earth) plane. There is always a method to their actions, whereby their deeper, ingrained responsibili-ty offers protection, security and guidance to their mates and loved ones. Feeding and giving shelter is considered their way of expressing love. They are romantic in an old-fashioned way, and seek to initiate relationships based on mutual respect and fair exchange. They usually inspire their partners to get ahead in the world, to make the best possible efforts they can for personal and professional suc-cess.

STRESSFUL ASPECTS TO PLANETS IN CAPRICORN:

Capricorn is concerned with their image in the world and social acceptance, and relationship and love needs some-times suffer as a result. Their calculated logic often leaves their partner feeling cold. Their resistance to go within and show true feelings (from polarity Cancer) often results in a hard exterior, but a very childlike interior. Stressful placements in Capricorn can result in severe discipline as their means of showing love.

AQUARIUS

"Whenever I call you 'Friend'
I begin to think I understand
Anywhere we are
You and I have always been
Forever and ever..."

Ken Loggins & Melissa Manchester
"Whenever I Call You Friend"

ELEMENT:	AIR
QUALITY:	FIXED
PLANET:	URANUS
HOUSE:	11 (FRIENDS, GROUP ACTIVITIES)
NATURE:	(+) humanistic, intelligent, people-loving, inventive, unique, futuristic, detached (−) eccentric, rebellious, scattered, cool, aloof, highly opinionated

WELL ASPECTED PLANETS IN AQUARIUS:

Aquarius combines its airy, people loving nature with the fixed mode of collecting. Thus, Aquarius collects people; they seek to form as many permanent or long-lasting relationships as possible throughout their lives. Because Aquarius is less concerned with personal love and more concerned with brotherly love in the purest sense, they connect with group activities and friendships. Adept at initiating relationships of all kinds, Aquarius is learning a detached, universal concept of love rather than personal, binding contractual relationships. They march to the beat of a different drum, and are attracted to mates or relationships that offer an intelligent way of expressing uniqueness. They are fiercely loyal friends and their mate will usually be friend first, then mate.

STRESSFUL ASPECTS TO PLANETS IN AQUARIUS:

Because of their strong need to be "right," along with an attitude that remains detached and resists showing feeling no matter what, an Aquarius with stressful placements has difficulty in maintaining one-to-one relationships. Restraints invoked by a partner will cause Aquarius to rebel because their need for freedom is so strong. Being electrical air, Aquarius has an extremely restless, nervous energy, and they approach their causes with intensity and vigor, often infusing all their energy into their projects until they are totally depleted. Pure Aquarian energy has a very difficult time relating straight from the heart. This is what their polarity, Leo, is teaching them since it is a sign that rules the heart. Stresses here may also result in an unwillingness to "give up" any old relationships or friendships they have, even while strongly committed to a current relationship.

PISCES

"I'm just a soul whose intentions are good
Oh lord, please don't let me be misunderstood..."

Benjamin, Marcus & Caldwell
"Don't Let Me Be Misunderstood"

ELEMENT:	WATER
QUALITY:	MUTABLE
PLANET:	NEPTUNE
HOUSE:	12 (SUBCONSCIOUS, CONFINEMENT)
NATURE:	(+) sensitive, sympathetic, compassionate, empathetic, mystical, artistic, visionary (-) martyr, escapist, habitual, excessive, directionless, wishy-washy

WELL-ASPECTED PLANETS IN PISCES:

The world of Pisces deals with sensitivity, compassion and love on the highest plane. Therefore, Pisces seeks to form relationships based on sympathy, understanding and trust. Mutable water suggests a wellspring of untapped emotion which flows freely in each relationship that is formed. Their strong points bring beauty and art, poetry and romance to a relationship. Tender and gentle, they will seek a mate who can give them sturdiness, but who also displays qualities of sensitivity as well. They seek to share the intimacies of their being with a partner, and will offer all of themselves to the relationship if they feel the partner is worthy of that trust.

STRESSFUL ASPECTS TO PLANETS IN PISCES:

In Pisces, the victim/saviour syndrome is strong. They feel they need to be saving someone or being saved in a relationship. They are looking for the "ideal mate" and never seem to find one. When stressed, Pisces produces a myriad of confusing images about who they are, what they are doing and where they are going. Seeking perfection and

harmony in the universe, Pisces will often ignore the physical reality they live in to escape to another sphere.
Many of their escape valves include products that offer temporary highs, but ultimately result in habit-forming addictions. Their unwillingness to make a commitment for fear
it would be a mistake often results in a wishy-washy, direc-
tionless existence in which nothing gets completed. When
planets are stressed in Pisces, tears, depression or isolation set in. Leaving them in their own little world is the
best the partner can do until they are ready to come out.
In the 12th House, the door is locked and the resident is
the only one with the key.

How the 12 Signs Interact

The 12 signs follow a never-changing sequence around
the wheel. Within this sequence is a built-in wave of Yang
(+)/Yin(-) interaction. What seemed important in one sign
becomes the antithesis of expression in the next sign.
Many are often surprised when upon discovering their horoscope, they find they have, for example, four planets in
Aries and were relating solely to being a Pisces. The personality planets Sun, Mercury and Venus always stay very
close together, never more than two signs apart. Most of
us have these three planets in at least two signs, if not
three, which are right next to each other in the zodiac.
The signs next to each other, although close by proximity,
are probably the furthest away from each other in personality types.

ARIES/BEING (+): At the beginning of the cycle, Aries is
concerned with being. Unlike its predecessor Pisces, who
was concerned with endings, Aries initiates. Where Pisces
looked within, Aries looks out. Where Pisces sought confinement, Aries needs room to explore.

TAURUS/HAVING (-): Settling down into fixed earth, Taurus
seeks to gather together and hold. Having come from Aries
who was spontaneous and initiating, Taurus prefers to settle in and consolidate. Where Aries moved fast, Taurus
prefers the slower pace.

GEMINI/THINKING (+): Coming out of the material phase of
Taurus, Gemini needs to experience the mind. Where Taurus
sought the physical realities, Gemini prefers the thinking
process. Where Taurus' range of experience seemed narrow,
Gemini's is dual and multi-faceted.

CANCER/FEELING (-): Coming out of the amusement park of
outer stimuli in Gemini, Cancer seeks feeling and nurturing
within. Where Gemini was superficial, exploring many,
Cancer becomes serious, exploring few. Where Gemini could
not make commitments, Cancer needs commitment. Where Gem-

ini wanted to talk, Cancer wants feeling.

LEO/ACTING (+): After an experience of an under-developed ego in Cancer, Leo seeks to emphasize the ego gratification needs. Where Cancer sought inner security through nurturing, Leo seeks public attention through acting. Where Cancer put up walls, Leo breaks them down. Leo takes the Cancer sensitivity into physical sensation.

VIRGO/PERFECTING (-): Leo chose to act, but Virgo prefers to analyze the actions. Where Leo's experience depends upon relations with others, Virgo feels the need to go within and process. Leo was bold and daring; Virgo chooses the safe, more rational approach. Where Leo emphasized play, Virgo focuses on work.

LIBRA/BALANCING (+): After being so engrossed with the workings of one's own mind and body in Virgo, Libra seeks to explore this in the partner. Where relationships were criticized in Virgo, they are idealized in Libra. Where the actions were assessed in Virgo, judgment is made in Libra.

SCORPIO/DESIRING (-): Having just left the safe, middle road of Libra, Scorpio now needs to plunge into the extremes. Where Libra was compromise and peace, Scorpio needs action and invigoration for stimulation. Where Libra judges the outer world, Scorpio rips through the layers to get to the core. Where Libra wanted balance, Scorpio needs extremes. Where judgment was made in Libra, the sentence is passed in Scorpio.

SAGITTARIUS/UNDERSTANDING (+): Having just come out of the tunnels of Scorpio, Sagittarius' essence is basking in the warmth of fire. Where Scorpio sought the depths, Sagittarius ascends to the heights. Scorpio was serious and intense; Sagittarians can't take anything seriously. Where Scorpio observed and held, Sagittarius blurts out and lets go. Where Scorpio sought to destroy, Sagittarius seeks to create.

CAPRICORN/TAKING RESPONSIBILITY (-): Having jus left the somewhat roaming and irresponsible phase of Sagittarius, Capricorn is intent on being responsible for his actions. Because Sagittarius was non-committal, Capricorn commits. Where Sagittarius was philosophical, Capricorn needs the practical realism of the earth. Where Sagittarius was likely to give it all away, Capricorn seeks to hold on to it for a rainy day.

AQUARIUS/REFORMING (+): Having conformed to all of society's demands in Capricorn, Aquarius is intent on reforming and breaking tradition. Where Capricorn was grounded and stable, Aquarius is eccentric and spontaneous. Where Capricorn sought the practical, risk-free methods, Aquarius dares to take chances and be different.

PISCES/BELIEVING (-): Unlike Aquarius who formed many relationships in a detached manner, Pisces forms few, but in an all-encompassing manner. Where Aquarius was cool, Pisces needs warmth. Where Aquarius was detached, Pisces chooses to hold on. Where Aquarius demanded freedom, Pisces needs confinement and isolation.

WHEN INVOLVED WITH
A PERSON WHOSE CHART
CONTAINS A
STRONG AMOUNT OF: BE PREPARED TO:

ARIES OR   - move fast - they want it NOW
FIRST HOUSE   - follow through for them
                           - be open to adventure and sudden
                             whims
                           - handle hot headedness or temper
                             flare-ups
                           - give them much attention
                           - play and romp
                           - take orders, as they like to
                             direct
                           - care for the ever-present child
                             within

TAURUS OR   - give priority to money, financial
SECOND HOUSE   affairs
                           - yield to strong opinions
                           - give physical (touch) embraces
                             frequently
                           - learn patience for slow movement
                             or inactivity
                           - satisfy indulgences

GEMINI OR   - change projects in mid-stream
THIRD HOUSE   - be on the move a lot
                           - live with ever-changing personali-
                             ties
                           - accept frequent indecision
                           - listen well, as they like to talk
                             and talk and talk
                           - accept their multi-faceted inter-
                             ests

CANCER OR   - confront feelings and show affect-
FOURTH HOUSE   tions openly
                           - be concerned with family matters
                             and attachments
                           - deal with drastic mood swings
                           - provide the security, protection
                             and nurturing they need
                           - deal with frequent pouting

**LEO OR
FIFTH HOUSE**

- say "I Love You" a lot
- shower them with affection
- let them direct/lead
- become involved with or at least supportive of their activities
- have lots of "friendly" competition
- accept their childlike behavior patterns

**VIRGO OR
SIXTH HOUSE**

- accept critical analysis
- focus indepth on one area
- be instructive, as they will listen carefully
- let them have some space
- get caught up in whirlwind projects
- handle their obsessive interests in work, health, diet, neatness or perfectionism

**LIBRA OR
SEVENTH HOUSE**

- give and take fairly and equally (share all)
- look at the other side of the issue
- see things in perspective logically, not emotionally
- make decisions, as their indecision is frequent
- have "round table" talks

**SCORPIO OR
EIGHTH HOUSE**

- handle extreme highs and lows
- get into heavy, deep discussions
- explore their psychic leanings
- accept obsessive behavior as normal
- accept their fixed, rigid opinions as fact
- let them do the controlling
- give them privacy and time to brood - they enjoy the pits

**SAGITTARIUS OR
NINTH HOUSE**

- handle roving, restless energy patterns
- follow through for them
- take risks, speculate
- give them space (they do not want to share everything)
- accept their exaggerated behavior patterns as routine
- handle bluntness of speech and action
- laugh at yourself

CAPRICORN OR TENTH HOUSE	- deal with their conservative more traditional approach
	- accept their image or career as the most important thing in their life
	- be a good provider and protector
	- let them organize
	- accept family programming ("Mom did it this way...")
	- help them express their feelings as it is difficult for them to do

AQUARIUS OR ELEVENTH HOUSE	- allow them plenty of room
	- accept their uniqueness and intellectual "superiority"
	- accept their difficulty in really feeling
	- accept their need for lots of people in their life
	- learn to deal with their high nervous energy and scattered energy patterns

PISCES OR TWELFTH HOUSE	- act spontaneously (their frequent indecision could drive you crazy)
	- be feeling-oriented as they express this the most
	- accept their quiet, reflective, serene moods
	- have meaningful, "feeling," therapeutic dialogues
	- accept frequent depression/misery/martyrdom

ELEMENTS AND MODES

The 12 signs of the zodiac are made up of four elements (fire, earth, air and water) and three qualities or modes (cardinal, fixed and mutable). Figure 2-4 shows the element and mode of each of the signs.

The Four Elements

The four elements which constitute the signs are fire, earth, air and water. Each element depends on every other one to function. We need all four for harmony and balance. When we lack an element in our charts, we draw people and experiences into our lives with large amounts of that element to compensate for our lack. We also instinctively respond to those of like elements with a similar rhythm.

Figure 2-4
The Elements and Modes Around the Wheel

THE FIRE ELEMENT: Aries, Leo and Sagittarius

Fire is defined by Webster (1981) as the "phenomenon of combustion manifested in light, flame and heat," (p. 427). The fiery element does induce warmth, light and energy that is spontaneous and direct. Thus, the fire element produces quick and immediate action with a passion for the creative essence. Fire people seem to live life to its fullest, seeking to encounter each new experience as an adventure, a "high." If properly fueled, fire can ignite and spread quickly, and at times burn out just as quickly. In relationships, fiery people tend to be extroverts who act out their impulses in an open, direct manner.

THE EARTH ELEMENT: Taurus, Virgo and Capricorn

The name for the physical planet on which we reside, Earth, carries a connotation of grounding, realism and stability. Earth people understand what they can see, feel, touch, taste or smell with their five senses. The introverted earth type seems involved with the physical realities surrounding oneself. The earth type is one who is grounded, stable, concerned with the physical body, the job at hand and the structure within which one lives. Unlike fire, whose actions are spontaneous, earth people use a more cautious approach, planning each move carefully.

THE AIR ELEMENT: Gemini, Libra and Aquarius

The invisible mixture of gases which composes our atmosphere is given the name air and is much like the thinking process it represents. You cannot see it or photograph it, but air and thought exist nevertheless. Air is associated with thinking and social interaction. Air people are the idea people and their socially prone nature will usually find them mingling and mixing with others who need their ideas. While earth types carry plans into physical reality, air people seem more suited to generating and dispersing ideas and concepts.

THE WATER ELEMENT: Cancer, Scorpio and Pisces

Water makes up 3/4 of the earth's surface and 90 per cent of the human body and is the substance of survival, of being. Like the plants and animals of this planet, we as humans depend on water (nurturing, feeling, emotion) for our growth. We can survive without food longer than we can without water. Water has long been associated with the subconscious and the feeling nature. It allows us to connect with the subconscious energies that motivate us. Water beings possess sensitivity and have the ability to understand life's processes – how we feel about things and how we relate to those feelings.

The Three Modes (Qualities)

The three modes that constitute the 12 signs are cardinal, fixed and mutable. They represent energy expressions in a three-stage sequence that relate to behavior patterns.

THE CARDINAL MODE: Aries, Cancer, Libra and Capricorn

The cardinal mode, sometimes called moveable, is just that. In its movement, it seeks to explore, create, begin, initiate and conceive. Not content or concerned with finishing, cardinal's principle motivation is, do it now.

Whoever said, "Don't put off until tomorrow what you can do today," likely had a preponderance of cardinal points in his chart.

Aries seems to express this cardinal energy in its purest form, combining the similar qualities of fire to that of the cardinal mode. While all four of these signs are cardinal, each expresses their cardinality through a different element: Aries through fire, Cancer through water, Libra through air and Capricorn through earth.

The cardinal personality has a lot of "shoulds" in his vocabulary - "You should do this, you should not do that." It seems easy for the cardinal individual to identify with and therefore try to solve everyone else's problems.

Cardinal-dominant individuals are those who are self-motivated, need to act quickly and need to be involved in an ever-changing arena of new experience. They normally do not tolerate obstacles, choosing to go around them or head into them. Once headed into the obstacles, they begin to lose interest and desire a new direction. Patience and caution are not their keywords, and those dealing with the cardinal personality will have a much easier time once they realize this.

THE FIXED MODE: Taurus, Leo, Scorpio and Aquarius

The fixed mode is a sturdy, unbending collective force that allows things to endure. The fixed signs are concerned with stabilizing what was begun in the cardnal signs. Often this results in the fixed personality being unable to stop mid-stream, change their modus operandi or yield to other's ideas and opinions.

Taurus seems to epitomize the fixed mode, as its earth-based quality has a great deal of similarity. The different elements through which the fixed mode is expressed are: Taurus through earth, Leo through fire, Scorpio through water and Aquarius through air.

The fixed personalities are intent upon doing it themselves in their own way. They feel their learning ground is hard work, experience and personal sacrifice. As a result, they do not do well with cardinal-dominant individuals who offer advice on how they "should" do things.

Fixed individuals show a great deal more caution and planning than do cardinal types and have the ability to focus their energies into one field of endeavor at a time. They need to see the fruits of their efforts, therefore, they work hard at whatever they do.

It is best to remember when living with a fixed personality that their narrow range of focus precludes them from believing anything if they cannot see it. You won't have much luck in changing their opinions about anything unless it is proven beyond a shadow of a doubt or they are convinced it is their idea.

THE MUTABLE MODE: Gemini, Virgo, Sagittarius and Pisces

The mutable mode brings flexibility and adaptability to any situation. The mutable mode is concerned with dispersing what was begun in cardinal and stabilized in fixed. Thus, mutable persons are concerned with transmitting information and understanding the whole process.

Gemini seems to be the purest expression of this energy, combining the air element, which is concerned with thinking, and the mutable mode. The four mutable signs and the elements they work through are: Gemini through air, Virgo through earth, Sagittarius through fire and Pisces through water.

Mutable individuals move in and out of experiences frequently as do the cardinals, but in this case they are more concerned with evaluating, understanding and analyzing the experience rather than initiating it. They are quite likely to spend their time reading, educating, thinking and communicating, sorting out all the experiences they have had.

They usually require a great deal of freedom or a broad spectrum in which to operate to satisfy their ever-present mental cravings. When living with a mutable person, remember they are simultaneously experiencing a multitude of hobbies, ideas and plans. Getting them to focus on any one thing may not be realistic. A strong point of mutable people is their ability to adjust to any environment quickly and easily by tuning in mentally to what it is offering.

A good routine to follow when evaluating a chart is to use the ten planets, the Ascendant and the Midheaven to register the elements and modes. Thus, in the chart you may find a preponderance of fire and mutable, giving a Sagittarian signature to the chart even when Sagittarius does not seem that highly emphasized by planets (see Table 4-1). This is also helpful when comparing two charts. You will often find a strong link between the two charts by elemental and modal breakdown.

THE HOUSES OF THE HOROSCOPE

The 12 houses of the horoscopic wheel correspond roughly to the 12 signs, that is, each house has a sign's energy influencing and operating within it. In making a distinction between the two, it may be easier to think of the signs as a psychological frame of reference (perhaps hereditary in nature) and the houses as the environment or setting. Both play a large role in determining one's make-up.

Whereas the signs compose the 365-day movement of the earth around the Sun (our calendar), the houses are based upon the daily rotation of the earth, or the 24-hour clock (see Figures 2-1 and 2-2). Because houses are based upon this 24-hour rotation, they are considered an earth-based influence and can be viewed as the practical experience or lessons we are learning on the earth.

Blending Signs with Houses

When defining house influences in the horoscope, blend the houses with the signs that naturally rule those houses. For example, if a chart has a planetary emphasis in Virgo in the 1st House, you must blend the sign Virgo with the sign Aries (natural 1st House ruler). The Virgo-prone traits of critical analysis, orderliness, efficiency and organization would directly affect how one transmits one's energy and how that process is viewed by others (1st House arena). One with Virgo in the 1st House might be considered a perfectionist who reflects those traits in personal appearance. Additionally, this person may spend a great deal of time in self analysis because Aries (self) is combined with Virgo (analysis).

If this planetary emphasis in Virgo is in the 4th House, the same qualities of orderliness, critical analysis and efficiency would apply, but instead of being the personal costume one wears, it will be an attitude that manifests at home (4th House arena). One with this placement will most likely have been highly influenced by a parent (4th House), for these attitudes and the response to them are really a response to that parent. Whether the person is extra picky and neat at home or a total slob depends upon the relationship and reaction to that parent who was extra picky about the house when the person was young.

Let's say this Virgo emphasis falls in the 7th House of relationships and partnerships. What kind of people would this individual look for in establishing relationships? They would most likely be Virgonian. Physically, they may look and dress the part, or be overly concerned with personal hygiene and cleanliness. Mentally, they will be precise, storing and processing information like a computer. Emotionally they may be somewhat dry, preferring the logical (Spock-like) approach.

Analyze each house of the horoscope this way, taking the natural house ruler and blending it with the sign that falls there. Many houses will have two and sometimes three signs working within them. Then they become more complex and depend upon a network of planetary energies from which an evaluation is made.

In astrology, the traditional areas to analyze regarding what you give to others and what you receive from them is assigned to Houses 1 and 7, the natural houses of Aries and Libra, along with their corresponding rulers. Houses 1 and 7 constitute a polarity as do Houses 2 and 8, 3 and 9, 4 and 10, 5 and 11, and 6 and 12. It is through these polarities we can understand relationship needs in astrology.

There are basically two ends of the spectrum in Houses 1 and 7. The First House dramatizes the self: personal identity, needs and desires, who and what one represents. If this house is receiving stressful aspects from other points in the horoscope, the individual might assert too much ego, selfishness and lack of compromise, having difficulty maintaining any relationship for very long. The 7th House of the horoscope dramatizes the basis for forming partnerships - what one seeks in a partner and what one can expect from a partner. If the 7th House is stressed, the person may also find himself not remaining in a relationship very long due to the inability to have complete cooperation from a partner. When the 7th House of one's horoscope is active, there is often an over-emphasis on doing anything that will please the partner. There might be an unwillingness to be assertive, with a heavy reliance on the partner to initiate and make commitments for the relationship. There can be an attitude of "I'll do almost anything to please my partner to keep peace and keep the relationship together" with a resulting silent hostility toward the partner for not giving this individual what makes them happy.

Although their methods are different - and this is an example of the extremes of these houses - the end result is the same for 1st and 7th House individuals. Both parties are continually asking why they have problems in relationships.

Each sign in astrology has a polarity, as does each house. Although considered opposites, these polarities are in fact one. House and sign polarities are like the head and a tail of a coin, or like a yin and yang force that operates to make up a whole. They are the antidote for one another. It is easy to see how these polarities dictate relationship needs in astrology.

If one has an over-emphasis of the 1st House principle, the solution to many of one's problems will come through the 7th House - embracing the opinions and attitudes of someone close to that person. If one has an over-emphasis of the 7th House principle, the solution will come through the 1st House - asserting oneself, standing on your own two feet and balancing what one "gets" from a partner with what one "gives" to a partner.

A very basic overview of the house polarities can be summarized as follows:

HOUSE 1: myself and my needs
HOUSE 7: partner and their needs

HOUSE 2: my values and resources
HOUSE 8: partners' and others' resources

HOUSE 3: conscious, reasoning mind (output)
HOUSE 9: higher, intuitive mind (input)

HOUSE 4: nurturing parent, home and internal needs
HOUSE 10: disciplining parent, society and external needs

HOUSE 5: personal love and attachments
HOUSE 11: universal love and detachment

HOUSE 6: physical and mental perfection: (form world)
HOUSE 12: spiritual perfection: intuitive and unconscious
          (formless world)

Assume we are working with the chart of someone who has an abundance of Scorpio/8th House prominent in the chart. This could be a person who is quite dependent upon the partner's resources for security and livelihood. On the opposite end of the spectrum is the person with a large amount of Taurus/2nd House prominence. This could be a resourceful person, capable of developing monetary potential through one's own skills and talents. If the two of these people were to join together in some kind of relationship, it might work rather well. If, on the other hand, both people had an emphasis of Scorpio/8th House and looked to the other's resources for their security and dependency, this could be a potential problem in the relationship. It does not have to be a problem, though. What is important here is that both parties feel their partner is contributing something in the way of money, support or resources to each of these individuals and to the relationship.

In many relationships, if one person's planets are emphasized in predominantly one hemisphere, it works well when the partner's planets fill out the empty hemisphere. The empty houses of the horoscope (those containing no planets) represent areas of life where the individual seeks fulfillment outside of oneself, either through people or outside experiences. When the partner's chart fills the missing houses, it is as if the person were feeling fulfilled or completed by the other.

Typically, there will still be one or two empty areas that the partner's charts do not fill for each other. Those houses will represent the areas both parties look outside of their relationship to complete. Obviously, one, two or even three areas like this are quite normal and quite acceptable, but when the partners find themselves looking outside of the relationship for almost one-half of their needs, they really are not being fulfilled by the relationship and typically will look elsewhere until the partnership eventually dissolves.

Relationships and the Houses of the Horoscope

For purposes of relationship analysis, the following details the people we encounter according to the houses of the chart. Many of these are taken from Rex Bills' The Rulership Book (1971). Houses in parentheses indicate the derivative house system from which the particular relationships are derived. In other words, the 4th from the 5th means that if you turn the wheel so that the 5th House is in the 1st House position, what was the 8th House is now the 4th House. This can be done with any of the houses.

This list is particularly helpful in determining emphasized relationships with others in looking at natal or composite charts. For instance, an 11th House emphasis in a composite chart might refer to the spouse's children (stepchildren) or a son-in-law and daughter-in-law, rather than the group or circle of friends with which a couple is involved.

43

1st HOUSE: self; friends of brothers and sisters (11th of 3rd); brothers and sisters of friends (3rd of 11th); grand-parents (4th of 10th)

2nd HOUSE: bankers, brokers; friends of the family (11th of 4th)

3rd HOUSE: sisters and brothers (specifically the first); neighbors; close relatives (cousins); children of friends (5th of 11th); friends of children (11th of 5th)

4th HOUSE: the protective (nurturing) parent; family in general; partner's parent (10th of 7th)

5th HOUSE: lovers; children (specifically the first); second brother or sister; friends of partner (11th of 7th)

6th HOUSE: aunts and uncles (3rd of 4th); co-workers, employees, domestic help, servants; doctor, nurse or health consultant; pets (small animals)

7th HOUSE: partnerships, both marriage and business (specifically, the first marriage); relation-ships in general with other people; second child; grandparents (4th of 4th); nieces and nephews (5th of 3rd)

8th HOUSE: friends of parents (11th of 10th); friends of employer (11th of 10th)

9th HOUSE: spiritual teachers, religious figures; second marriage; third child; grandchildren (5th of 5th); brother- and sister-in-laws (3rd of 7th); animals (e.g. horses, cattle)

10th HOUSE: the disciplining parent; superiors, bosses, authority figures; partner's parent (4th of 7th)

11th HOUSE: friends, groups, organizations; third mar-riage; fourth child; adopted or step-children (5th of 7th); daughter or son-in-law (7th of 5th)

12th HOUSE: enemies, adversaries; aunts and uncles (3rd of 10th); secret liaisons

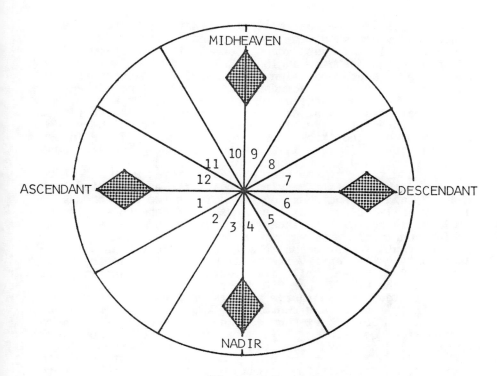

Figure 2-5
The Power Zones of the Horoscope

THE ANGLES AND AXES OF THE HOROSCOPE

The entryway or cusp of Houses 1, 4, 7, and 10 mark the angles of the horoscope. They are referred to as the Ascendant (ASC), Nadir (IC), Descendant (DSC) and Midheaven (MC) respectively (Figure 2-5). The Nadir is sometimes labeled the "I.C." on charts, while the Midheaven is often labeled the "M.C." on charts. These terms are Latin for Innum coeli and Medium coeli respectively. Marking the planets' rise, set, and upper and lower culmination, these four points define areas where planets' energies are strongest. Viewed as the "power zones" of the chart, look to 10 degrees either side of the angle for area of maximum potency. Both the principles of ASTRO*CARTO*GRAPHY (1976) by Jim Lewis and the statistical work of the Gauquelins (Cosmic Influences on Human Behavior, 1973) provide evidence of this principle.

The Ascendant/Descendant line is the horizontal axis that defines the horizon line in the chart. The Midheaven/Nadir line is the vertical axis that separates the eastern and western hemispheres (Figure 2-5).

An individual with planets falling on or near these

45

angles will derive the greatest strength from these placements as manifested in his own behavior patterns. If no
planets fall in these zones, look to the planetary rulers
of the signs on these angles. This is further intensified
when the planet and sign are located in these zones, for
instance, a Scorpio Ascendant with Pluto at the Midheaven.
Additionally, when others' planets fall on your angles, you
will feel the power of those particular planets with a
greater intensity. For instance, Prince Charles' Mars, Venus, Neptune and Moon are highly angular in Princess
Diana's chart (Figure 4-2), with Mars being the strongest
as it is only 1 degree from her ASC.

In addition to the four angles, reference is made here
to two other sets of angles: the Anti-Vertex/Vertex (AVX
and VX) and the East/West points. These two sets of angles
usually fall close to the Ascendant/Descendant axis and
will often coincide to those same points and angles in another's chart with whom we have a close association.

The Anti-Vertex seems to act in a similar manner to the
Ascendant. The Anti/Vertex will usually fall in the 12th,
1st or 2nd House, while its counterpart, the Vertex, will
fall in the 6th, 7th or 8th House. This axis will usually
be activated by another's planets or axes with whom there
are strong bonds and unavoidable (karmic if you will) encounters. (See Robert Hand's Planets in Composite for more
information concerning this principle.) Note Figure 4-4,
where the U.S.'s AVX is on the U.S.S.R.'s Midheaven and the
U.S.S.R.'s AVX is on the U.S.'s Sun and in exact square to
the U.S.'s Saturn. For a less volatile relationship, note
Figure 4-8, where Joanne Woodward's AVX conjuncts husband
Paul Newman's Venus, Mercury, ASC and Jupiter and Newman's
AVX conjuncts Woodward's Moon. Both the VX/AVX and the
East/West Points are calculated by most, if not all,
astrological computer services and programs.

The East Point (or equatorial ascendant) and its polarity the West Point (written as E and W in the horoscope)
are normally located 90 degrees from the Midheaven/Nadir,
and many times fall very close to the Ascendant/Descendant
axis. The East Point acts like an Ascendant and is usually
heavily aspected to a mate's chart. Note Figure 4-1 where
Charles's East Point conjuncts Diana's Sun.

The Nodal Axis and the Sun/Earth axis (the Earth is
always located 180 degrees from the Sun in a horoscope) is
the final set of polarities which constitute sensitive
points for us and will additionally be contacted by others
who have a strong part to play in our lives. For additional
information on the Moon's Nodes and the Sun, see Chapter 3,
"The Planets."

In summary, these six axes constitute potent energy
within the chart. I highly recommend using them in chart
analysis, especially in synastry. In looking at people's
charts who have had an important role to play in your life,
you will surely see these axes comingled and activated.
It's as if these axes are our invisible antennae sending
energy to and receiving energy from others. When others'
axes intersect ours, these antennae become stimulated and

46

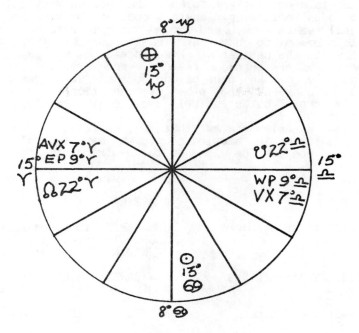

Figure 2-6

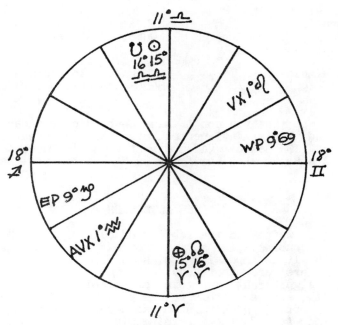

Figure 2-7

47

there is a need to get to know that person very quickly. I have been observing planetary contacts between couples for several years now, and I find among married couples it is quite common to have at least four of these six axes intersect the partner's. Even outside of marriage, between family members or close friends, these axes intersect quite frequently. When none of one person's set of axes correspond to any of the other's, the two people would most likely cross paths entirely unnoticed or unaffected by one another.

The example charts that follow (Figures 2-6 and 2-7) are those of a married couple who have several intersections by conjunction alone of these six points.

CHART A	CHART B
ASC/DSC 15 Aries/Libra	SUN/EARTH: 15 Libra/Aries
	NODES: 16 Aries/Libra
	MC/NADIR: 11 Libra/Aries
NODES: 22 Aries/Libra	SUN/EARTH: 15 Libra/Aries
	NODES: 16 Aries/Libra
MC/NADIR: 8 Cap/Can	EAST/WEST POINT: 9 Cap/Can
SUN/EARTH: 13 Can/Cap	EAST/WEST POINT: 9 Cap/Can
EAST/WEST POINT: 9 Libra/Aries	MC/NADIR: 11 Libra/Aries
	SUN/EARTH: 15 Libra/Aries
	NODES: 16 Aries/Libra
VERTEX/AVX: 7 Libra/Aries	MC/NADIR: 11 Libra/Aries
	SUN/EARTH: 15 Libra/Aries
	NODES: 16 Aries/Libra

Just so that you don't think Chart B's Ascendant/Descendant and Vertex/Anti-vertex are being ignored, Chart A's Mars at 18 Gemini falls directly on B's Descendant while Chart A's Venus at 5 Leo falls on B's Vertex at 1 Leo.

THE ASTEROIDS

While we're on the subject of points of strong contact between couples, let's not forget about the asteroids. Although it is impossible to use all the asteroids in chart work (there are thousands of them!), certain of them are highly significant in terms of relationships. I have not taken the space in this volume to include asteroids in the charts, but I highly recommend several books which can be consulted for further reading (see Bibliography). Worth mentioning, particularly in relationship to marriage, is

Juno, the symbol for marriage. In a study done in 1984 dealing with 106 pairs of married couples, contacts between Juno of one partner and the Ascendant of the other were extraordinarily high. Dr. Zipporah Dobyns has done much work with the original four asteroids, of which Juno is one.

Among some of the newer asteroids to emerge in the 1980's, I would recommend researching the positions and contacts of Eros, Sappho and Amor. All three have a strong part to play in love's many facets - devotional love, erotic love and spiritual love. The CAO Times publishes ephemerides for these asteroids (see Bibliography).

Chapter 3

THE PLANETS

CORE MEANING IN A CHART

In astrological charts, the planets are key ingredients. Everyone's chart contains all the planets operating through various signs. Although the 12 signs create a psychological backdrop for the planets, it is the planets which offer us the living, moving drama. We might simplify this as follows:

SIGNS:	The psychological attitude and expression	**WHAT:**	The Costume
HOUSES:	The arena or environment	**WHERE:**	The Stage
PLANETS:	The active role players or actors in the drama	**WHO:**	The Actors
ASPECTS:	The manner in which the planets communicate the dialogue with each other	**HOW:**	The Script

Because the planets are the active force or role players in our charts, the aspects between our planets and another person's set of planets constitute the script we will follow with one another. This, of course, is all done without a real script, but as if on cue, knowing instinctively how to respond to whatever planetary energies are coming our way from another.

POLARITIES BY PLANET

Just as each sign has a polarity, a yang (+) and yin (-) energy, so do the planets. Following is a suggested

51

listing of planetary polarities.

YANG (+) PLANETS	YIN (-) PLANETS
Sun	Moon
Mars	Venus
Jupiter	Saturn
Pluto	Neptune

Mercury and Uranus are considered neutral, being an expression on the mental plane and being either yang or yin at will. For more information on how a yin planet might act aspecting a yin planet or a yang to a yang and so forth, refer to the specific planets in question in the next section.

THE ASPECTS THEY MAKE

Aspects, as stated previously, constitute the dialogue of the chart. What the planets say, how they say it and the kind of response they get from one another are some of the issues raised by planetary aspects. Although aspects are only one of many elements viewed in analyzing a chart, they certainly are one of the most important in analyzing specific behavior patterns of an individual and are probably where astrologers place the most emphasis in chart delineations.

There are two types of aspects generally considered when viewing a chart. The major aspects (Figure 3-1) are almost always taken into consideration whereas the minor aspects are typically only considered after looking at the major aspects and sometimes only by those who feel they want to take the extra time to look at them. Because there has not been sufficient research performed on the importance of minor aspects, many astrologers do not use them. They are given here for consideration and research purposes for inclusion into horoscope analysis. I think ALL aspects are important because the fact that two planets are making any kind of aspect at all is often just as meaningful as what aspect they are making. An aspect of any kind establishes a communications link or dialogue between the two bodies, and that itself is important.

The question of aspect orbs needs to be considered when analyzing a chart. The tighter the orb is between two planets in aspect, the more significant the aspect. When an aspect is exact (for example, a 2 degree Taurus Moon to a 2 degree Scorpio Ascendant), there is a quick and immediate response. Looking at the horoscope of Mick Jagger (Figure 2-3), we notice five planets in Leo clustered around the Ascendant. The Sun at 2 Leo, the ASC at 4 Leo, Jupiter at 5 Leo and Pluto at 6 Leo would all come under the "conjunction" heading since they are within 10 degrees of one

Aspect	Location	Orb	Symbol

MAJOR ASPECTS:

Aspect	Location	Orb	Symbol
Conjunction	0°	10°	☌
Oppostion	180°	10°	☍
Trine	120°	6°	△
Square	90°	6°	□
Sextile	60°	3-5°	✶
Inconjunct	150°	3-5°	⊼

MINOR ASPECTS

Aspect	Location	Orb	Symbol
Semi-sextile	30°	2°	⊻
Semi-square	45°	2°	∠
Sesqui-square	135°	2°	⊡
Quintile	72°	1°	Q
Bi-quintile	144°	1°	BQ
Septile	51.5°	1°	S

Figure 3-1
The Aspects

another. Mercury at 11 Leo and the Node at 16 Leo are further away and while they are still conjunct the others and considered part of the stellium, they are not given the emphasis the first four planets were given which were so close together. Again, the smaller the orb, the more influence the aspect has.

Conjunctions, oppositions and close aspects of less than 2 degree orb are what I give the most emphasis in establishing the reaction of one individual upon another. Conjunctions are the cement by which the relationship is held together, while oppositions form the magnetic attraction and awareness one receives from another. Many individuals marvel at all the trines, sextiles, quintiles, etc. of a potential relationship, ignoring the fact that few, if any, conjunctions or oppositions exist. I use the opposition much like a conjunction, because the polarity shows two sides of the same coin. Additionally, the closest aspect in actual degree orb can be important in determining the effects of one person upon another. For instance, Jupiter in an individual's chart in exact (0 degrees, 0 minutes) semi-square to their partner's Saturn is an aspect of great importance in understanding the major theme of how this couple interacts, it being the closest aspect between the two charts.

Major Aspects

THE CONJUNCTION: (0 Degrees; allow up to 10 degree orb)

A conjunction occurs when two planets are within 10 degrees of each other. Usually the conjunction is in the same house and sign, but occasionally will occur in adjacent signs or houses. For instance, 29 degrees Pisces would be conjunct 5 Aries, yet there are two different signs. The 10 degree orb that I have allowed here is quite liberal, because I feel a conjunction is a powerful set of planetary energies, far more powerful than any other aspect (with the possible exception of the opposition). Therefore, a wider orb on a conjunction may be more meaningful than a closer orb on a trine or square.

The conjunction brings together two energy force fields that give birth to a pattern of thinking or behavior which encompasses the nature of both (or all) the planets involved in that conjunction in a most dynamic way. Opportunities are created and much activity occurs wherever the conjunction chooses to manifest itself. The planets that are conjunct do not operate in their "pure" form – they are a hybrid and become operative as a unit in their expression. The individual will usually seek out people and experiences that correlate to their planetary conjunctions, as they are always seeking to "marry" the two principles. Whether these two planets (or principles) are easily combined or compatible is another matter. The midpoint by degree and minute of a planetary conjunction will often be the highly sensitive point that becomes the release for these planets' energies.

In synastry too, the conjunction from one's planet or angle to another's planet or angle is extremely powerful and is the most potent energy operating. The two people are bound to have some kind of effect on one another. The closer the orb of the conjunction, the more impact they will have.

THE OPPOSITION: (180 Degrees; allow up to 10 degree orb)

The opposition is the second most powerful aspect in the chart after the conjunction. It is extremely significant in compatibility analysis, as people often use their partners to play out the opposition. The two planets or points which oppose each other on the wheel create a direct line of energy. With that energy is a powerful attraction, just like a magnet to steel, which often registers as quite stimulating when we meet people whose planets oppose our own. An opposition in a natal chart challenges one to integrate the two planets through the help and awareness of another person. The natal opposition often describes the kind of relationships one forms with others, whereby roles are unconsciously assigned to each individual to play out those two planets.

THE TRINE: (120 Degrees; allow up to 6 degrees orb)

Four signs apart, trines occur in the same element. A grand trine involves three planets or points, all within orb of 120 degrees apart, that connect to one another to form a triangle. While the grand trine has been referred to in the past as extremely fortunate, it can involve energy that is habitual and can often indicate a rut or syndrome into which the individual continually falls. A trine is considered an easy aspect, as it involves a talent or ability the individual brings with him. It is usually something that comes quite naturally, and may be considered luck or being at the right place at the right time. It does not necessarily stimulate growth or action. Too many trines can indicate lazy, habitual patterns which the individual does not desire to break, nor does he find a need to break. Many trines usually make for an easy-going, relaxed individual who is not in a big hurry to get anywhere. Trines do help ease the burden and offer the way out for a chart that contains many squares.

In charts between two people, planets that trine each other express a rhythmic pattern of harmony and will usually bring smiles to each other. In compatibility analysis, if one person's chart contains many trines and the other's contains very few trines but more squares, oppositions or hard aspects, it will be difficult for the two to understand each other's natural flow. The square personality is always looking for activity and trying to solve a crisis or create one. The trine personality has a tendency to relax and not go out of the way to create or solve anything. Therefore, the square person will wonder why the trine person doesn't do something and may accuse him of being lazy, while the trine person wonders why the square person gets upset over the small things all the time.

THE SQUARE: (90 Degrees; allow up to 6 degrees orb)

Three signs apart, signs of the same mode square each other. A square usually involves some inner stress and turmoil. Unlike the opposition, which brings another person or situation in for resolution, the square must be resolved internally. Squares create blind spots in one's nature. It is easy to see the reaction to a square, yet hard to locate the cause. Squares often challenge the limits of one's power and authority, or produce ego trips which go nowhere. People with many squares have a lot of physical drive and others can't or don't always desire to keep up with them.

When successfully worked through, the square offers reward and achievement. A square between two people's planets calls for a rechanneling of potent energy or strong wills that often results in conflict, but constitutes the dynamics of a relationship. When buttons are pushed by another, look at the squares between the charts and you will usually locate the source. For instance, if one per-

son's chart contains a natal square or T-square (a set of
three planets that form two squares and one opposition to
each other), another's planet contacting anyone of those
points will generally cause a powerful reaction. When someone says, "That person sure knows how to push my buttons,"
the buttons he's referring to are usually his T-square.
The trigger is often the other person's planet (or another
T-square) that contacts it directly.

THE SEXTILE: (60 Degrees; allow a 3 to 5 degree orb)

Sextiles occur between every other sign. Because it is
one-half the trine, the talent or gift offered by the trine
may not be fully developed, yet opportunities exist in
one's life to create those trines. The sextile personality
finds he has an abundance of choices available to him in
whatever he chooses to do, but he does have to do something. The sextile is an aspect that assists the personality in becoming sociable, talkative and outgoing. Between
two people, then, the sextile creates a positive, outgoing,
friendly mannerism.

THE INCONJUNCT/QUINCUNX: (150 Degrees; allow a 3 to 5 degree orb)

The inconjunct is a most misunderstood aspect. It
looks like a see-saw and people who have inconjuncts often
feel as if they are on one. It pulls in both positive and
negative qualities as it is halfway between a trine and an
opposition. It produces analyzing scheming and probing, as
the natural inconjunct starting from 0 Aries reaches to
both Virgo and Scorpio. Because of over-analysis, there
doesn't seem to be an easy solution. The pieces of the puzzle must be worked out carefully and diligently to produce
favorable results. These people are generally in analysis
most of their lives and are either trying to figure out
themselves or everyone around them.
The inconjunct often involves a very unusual nature or
personality, as the individual attempts to express two seemingly foreign concepts that don't readily integrate. An
example of this is the priest who wants to get married.
This aspect occurs frequently in the charts of people whose
parents have radically different ideas or backgrounds in a
specific area; the child born of this union must somehow
integrate these two elements. For instance, a Jupiter or
Sagittarius point in an inconjunct to another planet often
indicates two parents with radically different philosophical or religious outlooks. The child has both viewpoints
and his attempts to integrate them often result in an unusual manifestation. Because the elements and modes are
different, there doesn't seem to be an "easy solution."
The pieces of the puzzle must be worked with carefully and
diligently to produce good results. Usually, one with this
aspect will try to please someone else at the expense of

his true, inner nature, because if he does what he wants to do, others will be hurt. This can often result in guilt complexes. The best way to work with this aspect is to follow one's true conscience and inner voice.

Between two people, inconjunct aspects will be magnetic and appealing, but often hard to live with. Timing may be off between them as they operate on different rhythms. They may have to work hard to compromise with one another as their inherent perspectives differ. And, they must be careful about guilty feelings which will crop up from time to time, as their expectations of each other don't live up to what they had anticipated.

Minor Aspects

THE SEMI-SQUARE & SESQUI-SQUARE or OCTILE & TRI-OCTILE: (45 and 135 degrees or one-eighth and three-eighths of the circle; allow up to 2 degrees orb)

These two aspects are part of the square family, the semi-square being one-half the square and the sesqui-square being one-and-a-half squares. They act much like the square, except that in the semi-square, the pattern is just being developed, while in the sesqui-square, it is attempting to be released. The semi-square, therefore, does offer a bit less irritation than the sesqui-square since the sesqui-square has already been through the development of the square and didn't resolve it well. Because of the tension points and trigger buttons inherent in these aspects, they can create stress between two charts if there are many of them operating.

THE SEMI-SEXTILE: (30 Degrees; 2 degree orb)

Although this 30-degree aspect is pretty weak and powerless, it is helpful in charts that contain many inconjuncts as this is the aspect that provides the missing puzzle piece. A half of a sextile, the semi-sextile may go entirely unnoticed if an effort is not made to seize opportunities and develop them. It's as if the planets are sitting there waiting for each to acknowledge the other. They are both interested, but are too timid to make the first move because of possible fear of rejection.

THE QUINTILE & BI-QUINTILE: (72 & 144 degrees: 1 degree orb)

The quintile, a 72 degree aspect, is the result of the 360-degree wheel being divided by 5. Since 5 is a Mercury ruled number, this quintile series, like Mercury, operates on a mental plane. It has been referred to as the "genius" aspect and there is a talent working on this plane. A set of quintiles or bi-quintiles between two people would in-

volve an innate mental understanding of how the other individual operates and what motivates him/her. They may think
alike or have a very similar thought process.

THE SEPTILE: (51.5 degrees: allow up to 1 degree orb)

The septile is formed when the 360-degree wheel is divided by 7. The 7, being a Neptune-ruled number, prefers
to operate through the "inner planes" and results in a
subtler, more etheric energy. The septile produces an energy field which can be psychic and creative in its higher
manifestation, preferring the non-material reality. In its
negative manifestation, the septile, like Neptune, clouds,
confuses and deludes the situation so that vision is out of
focus. In charts between two people, the septile can bring
in a psychic connection, offering innate understanding, or
make one believe that the relationship is the way they want
to see it, regardless of the truth.

PLANET TO PLANET CONTACT BETWEEN CHARTS

My intention here is to briefly summarize the planets'
nature and principles rather than go on at length about
them. There are many good astrological textbooks (see
recommended reading list) that give in-depth descriptions
of the planetary symbols. My purpose is to create a feeling of the planets' role in determining love and relationship indicators. For this reason, the planetary descriptions are limited to those roles.

This section deals mainly with the chemistry that is
created by the interaction of two planets. Every possible
combination between the Sun, Moon, planets and angles of
the chart are discussed. These combinations are valid for
chart-to-chart comparisons between two individuals, in composite chart analysis or in natal chart analysis. Table
3-1 may be helpful in recording planetary aspects between
two people.

The bulk of this chapter deals with contacts between
planets, such as SUN/SUN, SUN/MOON, etc. I have not made a
distinction here between SUN TRINE SUN, SUN SEXTILE SUN,
SUN SQUARE SUN, etc. for two reasons. The first is that
many other textbooks do this. Secondly and more important
is that I feel there is little, if any, difference between
something like SUN TRINE SUN and SUN SEXTILE SUN, or the
difference is so subtle as to barely be appreciable. What
is more important here is that the SUN of one person is in
direct dialogue with the SUN of the other person. The
trine does not always insure a beautiful dialogue just as
the square does not always indicate a conflicting dialogue. However, the more dynamic aspects (0, 90, 180
degrees) create a stronger reaction one way or another than
the soft aspects (60, 120 degrees). I will leave it up to
the reader to weigh the particular aspect in question with

Table 3-1
Comparison Chart of Aspects

	☉	☽	☿	♀	♂	♃	♄	♅	♆	♇	☊	A Sc.	MC.	VX	EP		
☉																	
☽																	
☿																	
♀																	
♂																	
♃																	
♄																	
♅																	
♆																	
♇																	
☊																	
A Sc.																	
MC.																	
VX																	
EP																	

the other factors in the horoscope to determine how the energy is being used, allowing that any aspect from one person's planet to another's can result in constructive or destructive output and often does both at different times.

Several references are made concerning research done on married and/or divorced couples. For a full explanation of the research methodology and findings, please refer to Appendix A.

SUN

"You light up my life
You give me hope to carry on
You light up my days
And fill my nights with song..."

Joe Brooks
"You Light Up My Life"

RULER OF: LEO (5)   **PRINCIPLE:** personality, self-expression, vitality, personal identity, the father principle, creative expression

WHAT IT REPRESENTS:

The Sun is the yang (+) energy which symbolizes the father principle. The Sun is our outward expression, both natural and spontaneous, and represents how we act in public. It is the part of our nature that shines, our ego identity, and our ability to express ourself creatively. The Sun's vitality, energy and warmth are indicated by the way the Sun gives light and warmth to the earth. Growth would not be possible without it.

Someone else's Sun in our chart will light up that house (area of life) for us. For instance, someone's Sun falling in our 3rd House will spark our thinking. They may take an active role in our mental and educational development or stimulate and further our writing and speaking ability. We would likely spend hours on the phone with them in personal conversations, talking and exchanging ideas.

A close contact by conjunction or opposition to one's Sun is desireable, in fact necessary, for a relationship to be successful. In the research involving planetary contacts between couples (see Appendix A), the Sun of one partner is very often in close contact to the other's significant planets or angles. With Sun contacts, a relationship maintains its vitality, spark, enthusiasm and character. One problem occurring from too much Sun energy might be the overpowering or overshadowing effect, with one's Sun demanding and getting all the attention and the other standing in the shadow. The following is the reaction the Sun in one chart will have on another's planets or angles.

60

SUN/SUN

Similar qualities are recognized in each other. Goals, energy level and expression are similar and compatibility can be instant. Sometimes, when two people with Suns contacting come together in a challenging way, there will be competition or they might follow the beat of a different drum. Occasionally, the identification is too strong, and it will cause intense reactions to those parts of the personality that are not well integrated, creating ego conflicts. Generally, we will remember more distinctly people of either the same sun sign or when both Suns are in very close aspect to each other. Whether it is a powerful attraction or repulsion, there usually is no halfway point when this planet pair makes aspect.

SUN/MOON

Traditionally, it has been observed that this pair should be in contact with each other for a successful marriage because it is an ideal relationship between yin (-) and yang (+). Current research corroborates that it is a pair that shows up quite often in married couples. Even though their personalities are different, there is a powerful attraction at work between the Sun and Moon, complementing each other's natural, instinctive energy patterns very well. Because the Moon's light in our atmosphere is reflected light of the Sun, it typically finds its strength, power and sustenance through the Sun's rays. Thus, the Moon as archetypal yin seems to blossom and grow, basking in the light of the Sun's presence. By the same token, the Sun as archetypal yang will seem to have a fuller, richer purpose in life when the Moon becomes part of it, a mate so to speak, whose purpose completes and regenerates the other.

The Moon, of course, is the more sensitive of the two and is the one in this pair who most typically offers support, protection and nurturing. The Sun will be inspired by the Moon to take a more sensitive approach to every issue, and the Moon will pour feelings out to the Sun in a natural, flowing way. The Moon may also find its role to be more domestic while the Sun performs a more public role.

In aspects that do present a challenge, the Moon must be cautious of not over-reacting emotionally to the Sun's naturally assertive (sometimes aggressive) manner. Although the Sun person will instantly know how to push the trigger buttons of the Moon person, they usually find ways to resolve the issues easily and can do well together in most partnerships.

SUN/MERCURY

This planetary aspect is a very mentally and/or verbally stimulating configuration. The Sun stimulates Mercury's thought cells and Mercury seeks to understand and communicate about how the Sun likes to act. The Sun will most likely be the one doing while Mercury will talk or think about the issue constantly. This might be a problem if the Sun gets frustrated by Mercury's all talk and no action. The problem would be lessened if Mercury also had the Sun in the same sign or the Sun also had Mercury in the same sign, making both pairs conjunct. It is a highly stimulating teaching and learning combination.

SUN/VENUS

The Sun feels beautified by Venus' presence, as Venus is not only lovely to look at, but makes Sun feel more beautiful. Venus goes around beautifying and decorating the Sun's environment in some way. A strong attraction exists here. The Sun expresses what Venus likes (loves) and socially this pair would do well together. Looks, beauty, glamour and art would be dominant factors in their relationship. They would possess a certain aura of magnetism of which others would want to be a part. Shared interests include cultural activities, social obligations, theater, parties, the arts, pleasure and children; these areas may well be where this combination finds the most compatibility. If there are any problems with this pair, it will likely be selfishness, as both tend to be spoiled and want to be indulged by one another.

SUN/MARS

Energy Plus! It's hard to know who makes the first move in this relationship because both will move fast, especially around each other. The Sun rules Leo and Mars rules Aries, two yang (+) planets operating through forceful, dynamic signs. These planets combine to arouse and stimulate each other's passions. Mars is animus, the activated, agressive force, whereas the Sun is ego identified with a strong personality of its own. A tendency to demand attention from each other is quite possible with this aspect. There is a high sexual and physical drive associated with these two planets acting together which may be best expressed through physical closeness, sports, fitness and so forth. Mars might push or prod the Sun which could cause the Sun to feel a bit insecure at times, as Mars's unbridled energy can be harsh. With this aspect prominent in the two charts, the "little child" will often come out to play. The soft aspects would create similar energy patterns and shared interests might include running, aerobics, dance and, of course, all sexual activities. The martial arts is another area where these two might find a similar outlet of expression.

SUN/JUPITER

This is generally an aspect that promotes happiness, a sense of expansion and public good between two people. A good business relationship exists here from the aspect of promotion and public relations. Jupiter promotes (and often exaggerates) the qualities and attributes of the Sun person. Jupiter is a giver. The Sun in turn would feel blessed by Jupiter, and would tend to reciprocate. Control may be needed here not to overdo, overspend or overindulge. They may get so used to each other's giving natures that they come to expect things from each other, often resulting in selfishness. The combination in a stressful aspect could produce an inflated sense of self importance to each individual and the couple. But more often than not, the Sun and Jupiter experience a beneficial relationship with one another.

SUN/SATURN

A typical reaction to someone's Saturn on someone else's Sun is for the Sun person to claim that Saturn inhibits the Sun's natural, free-flowing energy. Yet there is a strong attraction, especially in situations where one is seeking to form a business partnership or be instructed and disciplined in some way by the other.

The Sun and Saturn both represent parenting in general and fathering, more specifically. Thus, the combination enhances two people who are part of a family unit (husband, wife, parent, child, siblings, etc.). Sun/Saturn is a very good combination in teaching, family or personal counseling and business associations. Saturn's role is to offer form, structure and discipline, so its effect will be to parent or take care of the Sun person with a great amount of pride and personal attachment to the outcome.

In the challenging aspects, Saturn may rain on the Sun's parade. Saturn's method would be, "Grow up - become responsible for your actions." The Sun, acting as the child, would seem to be more concerned with play and free-flow expression. Saturn will sometimes stifle or inhibit the Sun from acting freely and spontaneously. The Sun will often make light of what Saturn works hard for and takes seriously. Vulnerability is, at times, depicted through Saturn's position in the chart. With the Sun shining its light on that area, Saturn may always feel somewhat insecure in this relationship, feeling that the Sun is _always_ focusing on his weak points, and never seeing the good that Saturn does.

SUN/URANUS

A natural sign polarity occurs here because the Sun is ruler of Leo and Uranus is ruler of Aquarius. It is a magnetic attraction that is highly charismatic. Therefore, a carefree, spontaneous type of relationship works best between these two planets.

This planetary contact would show the urge to express uniqueness, individuality and higher intelligence with a little bit of insanity thrown in. In other words, a Sun/Uranus contact in a couples' chart might encourage each person to be oneself, to express one's uniqueness without fear of judgment from the other person. In fact, the wilder and crazier the personality expression, the more the partner might encourage such expression. The major challenge here is that the Sun, ruler of Leo, wants strokes and lots of attention, while Uranus, ruler of Aquarius, stresses detachment as a way of life. Additionally, the Sun plays the parent role, wanting to protect and care for the partner, while Uranus is often the rebellious child, wanting to do things his own way. The aspect between these two planets will cause change, one way or another, and will force the Sun to look at things in a new light.

SUN/NEPTUNE

There is a poetic, romantic activity or expression that brings these two together. Here is a yang (+) Sun combining with a yin (-) Neptune to create a balanced flow. This combination is beneficial in psychic development, spiritual training, musical, artistic or poetic interests where Neptune expresses itself best. Neptune's dreamy, illusive quality can inspire the Sun to act out his own dreams and creations.

Neptune sensitizes the Sun into a mystical type of relationship involving deep, emotional feeling. Both are creatively inclined, with Neptune being tuned into higher channels of awareness and the Sun seeking to actively express his creativity. In relationships that do not seek these creative channels, the influence can be one of dishonesty, deceit or the victim/saviour syndrome between the two people. Another danger can be escaping on their magic carpet, only to wake up and find out no one was at the controls or the pilot was drunk. Yet, this relationship seems to be one both people feel is cosmic and made in heaven, as Neptune seems radiant from bathing in the Sun's rays.

SUN/PLUTO

Pluto acts as a transformer, and a close conjunction between these two will ultimately change the Sun's life and alter his expression. There is a powerful force connected here with solar energy (Sun) and atomic power (Pluto) coming together to elicit very strong reactions. All hard aspects between the Sun and Pluto can be attractive but highly volatile. The two planets represent signs (Leo and Scorpio) which form a natural square to each other. Both signs like to remain in control of themselves and their environment. Pluto has a powerful effect upon the Sun, yet it is a two-way circuit here, as Sun shines its rays of light upon Pluto's innermost, submerged feelings and seems to know exactly how to bring them to the surface. This planetary combination is effective in therapy, healing and the personal transformation two people seek in a relationship. They will share their innermost secrets, seeking a possessiveness with each other, but will also need space from each other if it gets too intense (and it does).

SUN/NODES

The North Node is sociable and loves organizing events and directing people, so the connection to the Sun would be favorable for gain, popularity and publicity. Both the Sun and Node are considered friendly in nature. Couples with this contact would tend to do well together in a work relationship. The Sun is already acting out and expressing what the North Node is developing. A prominent association between the Sun and Nodes occurs frequently in families. Sun/North Node contacts are also favorable for people who share the same hobbies and professional concerns.

Sun/South Node contacts will seem destined. They remind each other of something or someone from their past. They usually don't need an introduction because when they see each other, they feel they have already met. The Sun, though, will take the lead because the South Node is a little more reserved and deep in feeling. The South Node is always the receiver in any planetary pair, and with the Sun's rays shining upon it, it is usually receiving something beneficial from the Sun person.

SUN/ASCENDANT

Sun/ASC and Sun/DSC contacts show up frequently between two people in almost every kind of relationship. If one has the Sun in Gemini, for instance, there will be a strong attraction to, and friendliness and personal identification towards one with Gemini and/or Sagittarius rising. The Ascendant is the personal doorway to the self in the chart (who am I), whereas the Sun is the personality expression (how do I act). They have a lot in common, as the Sun acts out who the Ascendant is.

The Ascendant marks the time one enters the world, and as a soul energy, what is actualized as one grows and matures. The Sun helps the Asendant express this and the Ascendant often helps the Sun get started. This is a combination that will find many mutual interests, similar personalities and active concern and participation with each others' lives.

SUN/MIDHEAVEN

Like the Sun/Ascendant, there are usually many close aspects between Sun/Midheaven couples. Both are concerned with how they look and act in public, the Sun being how we act and the MC being what society thinks of us in addition to what we're striving towards. Both have an association with the parent role with the MC being a parental point marking the beginning of the 10th House and the Sun ruling Leo (5) expressing the father principle. Generally, this combination produces a smooth running relationship, where both are acutely aware of each other's status and progress in the world. Since the MC is not a planet but a point, it acts more as a receiver with the Sun shining its rays upon it. Therefore, the Sun person would tend to be the active force in this relationship and make the MC feel good about what he is doing or not doing professionally or publicly.

MOON

"And all the night's magic seems to whisper and hush
And all the soft moonlight seems to shine in your
   blush.
Can I just have one more Moondance with you, my love?
Can I just make some more romance with you, my
   love?..."

Van Morrison
"Moondance"

RULER OF: CANCER (4)   PRINCIPLE: nurturing, the
                               mother principle, inner feel-
                               ings, sensitivity, domestici-
                               ty, emotions

WHAT IT REPRESENTS:

As the Moon reflects the light of the Sun and shows us its shape and color through that reflection, so too will the Moon in our chart take on the shape and color of its sign, house and aspects. The Sun represents the yang (+) active force or father principle, whereas the Moon represents the yin (-) reactive force and mother principle.

The Sun represents the daylight force in our lives, while the Moon governs the nighttime force and often promotes responses from an inner feeling level. On a subconscious level, the Moon guides and directs us in choosing what appeals to us, what makes us feel good and what motivates our inner urges for contentment. It is our daily habit patterns which we developed in early childhood and carry into our adult lives. The Moon in our charts not only tells much about whether we felt nurtured, protected and loved in childhood, but also tells of our ability to pass along those same nurturing, protective and loving qualities to others as we grow and mature.

What may be most important about the Moon, however, is the influence it carries in our private and home lives. Often the partner with the strong Moon contact is looking to be mothered or looking to mother their mate. Moon contacts from another's chart usually indicate a receptivity, understanding and instinctive protection that person is offering. In relationships and especially cohabitational situations, the Moon is of utmost significance. If the Moons of a couple are not "happy" with each other, the relationship could be in deep trouble. The following combinations will show the significance of the Moon in one chart acting upon planets and points in another's chart.

MOON/MOON

Two people with this contact may feel like family together right from the start. They generally can peel off the outer layers and get right to the heart of things, possessing an innate ability to understand each other's psyches. The Moon's tendency is to mother and protect, so if the Moons are making a strong contact, both parties will seek to play that role. In a comfortable aspect, they would both enjoy living together and playing out a family role. In an uncomfortable and threatening aspect, they would tend to react emotionally to the smothering type of mothering that each would be prone to with one another. In relationships in which "mother" buttons are pushed, it is usually due to a lunar contact.

There is a great ability to understand and respect each other's sensitive areas – to a point. The conjunction of the Moons is almost non-existent for people that choose to live together, as opposed to those who have no choice about living together, (for instance, family members). When two Moons are conjunct, moodiness in both individuals occurs simultaneously and they seem to demand from, rather than give attention to, one another. The aspects the two Moons make are critical factors in determining the longevity and livelihood of a cohabitational relationship.

MOON/MERCURY

Close aspects between one person's Moon and another's Mercury are instrumental in getting a relationship off the ground. There is a high degree of Moon/Mercury aspects occurring in long-term couples. It is a "tuned-in" combination, as the Moon is always receptive and responsive to Mercury's thought-waves and ideas. The Moon helps Mercury understand intuitive functions, how to feel rather than rationalize emotions, how to quiet the nervous system and steady the mind. Mercury would steer the Moon into rational activity based on logic, not emotions. There is usually a highly developed telepathic rapport here because Mercury/Moon is a natural sender/receiver combination. The danger

here is that the Moon's feelings can get hurt too easily by
Mercury's apparent lack of feelings. This combination
would probably enjoy arguing for the sake of argument,
although never seriously - usually the cat and mouse type
games. There is a sense of friendly competition here when
the two people are working or playing together, each one
trying to outdo the other.

MOON/VENUS

A highly romantic, intuitive contact, these two seem to
enjoy each other's company immensely. The conjunction and
opposition appear frequently in almost every kind of close
relationship. Venus appreciates and understands what the
Moon feels, and together they can share a non-threatening
type of intimacy with each other. The Moon wants to nurture and care for Venus, while Venus loves the attention
and responds with love and affection. Couples with this
contact will often share many hobbies and interests, and
are usually very good roommates. They can immediately tell
when the other person is off-center or when something is
not right. The main warning here is that Venus could be
flirtatious, taking the Moon's feelings a bit too lightly
whereas the Moon's tendency would be to take things seriously. There is a highly sensitive and caring lovemaking ability between these two.

MOON/MARS

There is an intense physical or sexual magnetism that
brings these two together. The Moon feels and responds to
the high physical and emotional drives stimulated by Mars.
The attraction is usually sudden and quick. The danger
here is Mars can run roughshod over the Moon's sensitive
feelings. The Moon can sensitize Mars into a more polished
and tactful way of being unless the Moon is too strong and
domineering. If that is the case, Mars will fizzle out and
no real direction will be maintained. The Moon would react
to Mars's lack of drive in this case. The Moon generally
wants a lasting relationship, whereas Mars is only thinking
about today.

MOON/JUPITER

This pair highlights the Moon's rulership over Cancer
and Jupiter's exaltation in that sign. The Cancerian elements such as the sharing of family activities, food and
feelings would be highlighted with this contact. Many
couples choosing to live together have this aspect strongly
operating between the two charts. The Moon would instinctively feel nurtured by Jupiter's natural abilities for
optimism and good will; Jupiter would tend to indulge the
Moon's cravings on an emotional level. This combination

would most likely be fairly active in family affairs. As Jupiter's keyword can be too (much of anything), the danger here lies in a too self-indulgent relationship, where laziness or concern with physical and emotional appetites is dominant. Yet Jupiter would have a sense of optimism and friendliness that the Moon could reflect in a most positive way. The Moon must be careful not to get its feelings hurt by Jupiter's bluntness of speech and action.

MOON/SATURN

There is a natural polarity here, bringing together the rulers of Cancer (Moon) and Capricorn (Saturn). This relationship will often start with family issues being the dominant theme for both individuals. Saturn is reminded of Mom or Dad when encountering the Moon for the first time, so in one sense, there is a comfort based on familiarity. However, it is a difficult combination in any chart (natal, synastry, composite, etc.).

In a pleasant Moon/Saturn contact, typically the two sets of parents will like each other and "approve" of their child's partner, accepting them into the family wholeheartedly. There is a great deal of parenting that goes on with these two. If there are children of this partnership, they usually get the greatest amount of attention, and the partners often neglect to spend time alone with each other. If there are no children, the partners tend to parent each other or attempt to help each other solve family problems.

Any difficulty in this combination is usually experienced by the Moon to a greater degree, because the Moon likes free flow of expression, feeling, sensitivity and care, while Saturn cautions and has a natural tendency to reserve and inhibit such expression. Two yin planets, Saturn and the Moon both have a tendency to complain, worry and hold on to guilt, so care must be taken that a tendency to depression, moodiness or worry isn't the prevailing theme of this relationship. What is lacking in the relationship rather than what it has going for it can often be the issue.

This pair often compares their relationship to what society or family expects from them. This keeps them working toward an outer reality that doesn't bring fulfillment from within. If this is the strongest or most isolated contact between the pair, they will experience difficulty surviving a long-term relationship.

MOON/URANUS

This can be a highly charismatic aspect between two people with the Moon feeling and Uranus attracting. Uranus will usually be the one to initiate the relationship, as the Moon will often be too shy to make the first move, even though the Moon is dying for something to happen here. Since the Moon (Cancer ruler) and Uranus (Aquarius ruler) represent a natural inconjunct, this combination can be a rocky road at times. Both planets go through rapid mood changes and instability. Uranus plays a more mentally detached role, whereas the Moon wants to explore feelings and doesn't like to be ignored. They both tend to be easily excitable and don't stay with one mood for very long. The conjunction or close aspect here promotes rapid change, so the difficulties will be short-lived. This one is another freedom (Uranus) versus closeness (Moon) syndrome.

MOON/NEPTUNE

An extremely high percentage of couples in love have this contact. The Moon and Neptune are two yin water planets that can produce a very close personal, intimate relationship that is expressed much more in private than in public. This is often a relationship that seems like a soul connection right from the start, with both the Moon and Neptune loving and living in fantasy much of the time. Both believe in fantasy and see things the way they want to see them most of the time, regardless of the facts. Yet the quality of feelings and closeness one arouses in the other cannot be denied. They would tend to be very gentle and soothing to each other, allowing poetry, song and art to add magic to the relationship.

MOON/PLUTO

The Moon likes to protect and nurture and Pluto likes to possess and control. This can be a wonderfully intense relationship if both are used to possessing and being possessed in love. It is an aspect best suited to those loving and living together. In long-term married couples, hard aspects between this pair are quite frequent. As with Moon/Neptune, Moon/Pluto are two watery planets that can stir up depths of feeling never dreamed of by others. In this case, Pluto does the stirring and the Moon gets stirred. The reaction is sometimes favorable and sometimes not, as the Moon's sensitive feelings are always at stake and seem to get dredged up from deep water by Pluto. This combination will often include scenarios involving a need to work out jealousy on both their parts. It can produce a relationship that is secretive, volatile and changes both parties.

People with this aspect living together not by choice (siblings, parent/child, co-workers, etc.) may find themselves resenting each other and creating power plays to get more breathing space from one another. It is an aspect that seems to work best among lovers since there is such an intense sexual encounter going on. They seek to get as close as possible to each other and transform themselves through the sexual aspects of the relationship. People with this aspect have often remarked that "it was the best

70

sexual relationship" they've ever had with another person.

MOON/NODES

Extremely high percentages of hard aspects occur between the Moon and its Nodes in couples who are together. The pull to bring these two people together happens at such a powerful unconscious level that the two people seem to have no choice about the matter. They become a part of each other's lives, like it or not. They must like it, though, because it occurs in a very high percentage of long-term married couples. When the Moon and <u>South</u> Node are conjunct between two people, an emotionally stimulating relationship that has roots in the past is occurring. Both people connect to one another intuitively and psychically almost immediately. Chances are good that both these people express a similar emotional pattern and can readily identify with one another. The Moon conjunct the <u>North</u> Node stimulates future growth and development in a positive way, although there will still be an intense emotional involvement between the two people. The connection here is usually immediate and they both seem to know all about each other without having been told. The South Node is often looking for the Moon to play a "mother" role in their life, because they find the relationship with their own mother unfulfilled. This is usually fine with the Moon as it instinctively does well with the mothering role. The two are intuitive with one another. It is a combination that occurs frequently among family members or people who instinctively respond to and become involved with the other's family.

MOON/ASCENDANT

There is strong personal identification here based on feelings of nurturing. The Moon seeks to provide a nurturing, protective role for the Ascendant, while the Ascendant can't seem to forget the effects the Moon has had on him, no matter how brief the encounter. The Moon already feels and reflects for the Ascendant what the Ascendant is seeking to actualize. There is a strong connection here, as if it were a family tie, and the relationship can intensify one or both partners' own mother or the mothering role the Moon plays. The aspect occurs a great deal between parent and child, especially mother and child, but often it is the child who is the Moon (playing the mother role) and the parent who is the Ascendant (playing the child role).

MOON/MIDHEAVEN

This combination is suggestive of the Cancer/Capricorn polarity, as was Moon/Saturn, but these two usually take a lighter approach to the same situation. A strong parent, protector role is being played out, where the Moon is prodding the MC toward his own ambitions. Similar to the mother who encourages her son, the doctor, to achieve fame and fortune to further enhance her own needs for security, the Moon stimulates the MC to achieve a high degree of recognition for the Moon's own personal interests. Whatever kind of relationship that does exist between these two (lovers, friends, co-workers, etc.), they will act like family and feel a kinship or blood-tie with each other whether one actually exists or not. They tend to take the bad with the good and chalk it up to experience.

MERCURY

"Everytime I tried to tell you
The words just came out wrong
So I'll have to say I love you in a song..."

Jim Croce
"I'll Have to say I Love You
in a Song"

RULER OF: GEMINI (3)
     VIRGO (6)

PRINCIPLE: verbal exchange, the conscious and reasoning mind, logic, mental thought processes, communications, analyzations of all kinds

WHAT IT REPRESENTS:

As ruler of Gemini, Mercury is the talker. As ruler of Virgo, it functions as the thinker. Either way, thinking and communicating in one form or another is Mercury's key function. As a neutral planet, neither yin nor yang, Mercury articulates a process of reasoning, rationale and analysis that is important in all forms of human behavior. Because Mercury is considered neutral and absorbs quickly, it is said to take on the coloring of the sign and house position it occupies, along with aspects made by other celestial bodies. Mercury is our own individual process that involves many steps, taking only seconds to complete:

1. Hearing or seeing something explained
2. Absorbing and understanding it
3. Putting it into our own words
4. Transmitting that information to someone else
5. Making ourselves understood to that person

Although this seems like a very simple process, it is difficult to accomplish without distortions along the way. This makes Mercury a key factor in relationships. Are we communicating our desires and needs clearly to our partner and if we are, are they understanding our message? In a relationship, then, it is nice to have beneficial Mercury contacts. Lois Rodden's book The Mercury Method of Chart Comparison begins by stating, "Mercury opens the gates between two people." Indeed, if we can't communicate with or understand one another, a relationship becomes quite difficult to maintain. The following is Mercury's relationship to other planets it contacts in a chart.

MERCURY/MERCURY

Close aspects between these two indicate a verbally and mentally active relationship in which communicating to each other on a steady basis is of utmost importance, regardless of whether or not you agree. With the conjunction, the two people tend to think alike or share an interest they will want to exchange information about constantly. Often the two people's energy level and nervous systems vibrate at a similar frequency, and understanding is immediate. With the square, there is a challenge, almost a competitiveness between the two to understand each other. The opposition may automatically set up a pattern whereby both parties debate every issue, regardless of whether or not they agree. The inconjunct (150 degrees) is one of the most difficult. Here there is not only the challenge presented to understand each other, but an unwillingness on the part of both to make that effort to change their way of thinking. The soft aspects (trine, sextile) offer a smoother flow in most cases. Whatever the aspect, this combination enables two people to learn from each other and has more than just a passing interest in mind games.

MERCURY/VENUS

Intelligence meets beauty. They talk, they laugh, they love in togetherness. Mercury thinks or talks about what Venus loves, so there is a focus on where the compatibility does exist rather than where it does not. Research shows good friends and people we choose to socialize with, as well as people we choose to marry and live with, have strong Mercury/Venus contacts, often two ways (Mercury on one person's Venus and Venus on the other person's Mercury). This would be the one person you seek out in a crowded room or the co-worker in whom you take a personal interest.

MERCURY/MARS

These two can stay up all night long just talking to each other. They love fun and play lots of games, enjoying the competitiveness the games offer. Mars usually takes the initiative in this relationship and is stimulated by Mercury's eagerness to "play." Work activity and intellectual stimulation can occur quite easily.

A few problems may emerge with this pair. They both have a tendency to scatter and disperse energies (rulers of Aries and Gemini). This could result in hard hit but short-lived activity. Touchiness will occur if Mercury threatens Mars's sense of virility or Mars threatens Mercury's intellectual abilities. But probably the most exaggerated form of behavior that can occur between these two in a stressful relationship to one another is the tendency for arguments, yelling and screaming, with a hot-headed Mars meeting a vocally proficient Mercury.

The more positive usage of Mercury and Mars is the ability to find many outlets and shared interests that both individuals love. The combining of work and pleasure is easy. Because Mercury is a thinker and Mars is an energy expender, they can usually solve problems and analyze situations that need solving or repairing in an expedient manner. And of course, thought and conversation are highly stimulated between Mercury and Mars.

MERCURY/JUPITER

Mercury and Jupiter, when combined, stimulate thoughts, ideas, and conversation between two people, creating an environment where open communication is encouraged. A high occurrence of all kinds of aspects between Mercury and Jupiter is prominent in long-term married couples. These two are a natural polarity (rulers of Gemini and Sagittarius respectively) and focus on mental and intellectual interchange. One always wants to ask questions and the other likes to answer them. They can feed off of each other's stimulating mental patterns for quite some time. They tend to feel they are together to teach each other and learn from each other, but their approaches are slightly different. This is often the pair that meet in a classroom situation.

Jupiter helps give Mercury's conscious mind a chance to broaden its horizons, and at the same time helps Mercury set goals for all its ideas. Mercury helps Jupiter put things in perspective, enabling a more realistic viewpoint. Generally, this aspect is an open, spontaneous and friendly union, as both planets complement each other's innate natures. They have a great mental attunement towards each other and when they are together, there seems to be excitability in the air. They love to talk (Mercury) a lot (Jupiter), and may make others in their sphere feel "left out" at times.

MERCURY/SATURN

The attraction between this pair is often based on Mercury's attempts at learning and disciplining its skills, and Saturn's ability to teach and discipline. However, Mercury can feel inhibited around Saturn because Saturn seems to require strict discipline of the mind and concentrative faculties that Mercury may not have well developed yet. They really have a need to learn something from each other, which is why they're both together. With Saturn's influence nearby, the conversations will tend to be serious more often than not. Mercury may have a hard time verbalizing or communicating what really needs to be said for fear that Saturn will make fun of or pass judgment on Mercury's message.

In harmonious contacts, this relationship should help the two organize and analyze projects, bringing together Mercury's rulership of Virgo and Saturn's of Capricorn. It can also be a highly intelligent contact that, when given a job, can put their heads together to do incredible work.

MERCURY/URANUS

Similar to Mercury/Jupiter, this is a highly intellectual combination. Both of these mentally active, neutral planets offer stimulating thought and focus on a non-physical type of relationship. Watching these two toss ideas, concepts and philosophies back and forth is much like watching an exciting, championship tennis match. A high degree of telepathy occurs here as Mercury is an exceptional sender and Uranus an acutely aware receiver. Vibrational and nervous system activity is highly stimulated with this pair in close aspect, as if they are on some artificial stimulant all the time. They get excited in each other's presence and always need to share. There is rarely a misunderstanding here - maybe an unwillingness to accept the other's viewpoint, but nevertheless, the message is received.

MERCURY/NEPTUNE

When Mercury, the ruler of mutable Gemini and Virgo, meets Neptune, the ruler of mutable Pisces, the result can be diffused, confused messages. They both expect perfection. Since rarely, if ever, is anything perfect, there is often a sense of loss or unattainableness in the relationship. There is, however, the ability to sympathize with and be compassionate toward one another.

Mercury wants to talk and share feelings, while Neptune finds it hard to verbalize. This is often a source of misunderstanding on the part of both, because when Neptune doesn't communicate, Mercury withdraws and they both assume the other is feeling or thinking something that really is not happening. This can be the case where one or both of them expects the other to know what they are thinking or feeling, to read their mind. But both can be afraid to ask and get clarity on the matter. With Mercury desiring clear communications and Neptune having a hard time focusing, there may be a frequent occurrence of "I don't understand you" or the more likely "You don't understand me" scripts being played out.

In harmonious aspects there is a stimulation of the feeling sense or a merging of the minds. Neptune might be able to offer Mercury a chance at calming its busy mind, in turning it towards more creative and artistic channels, perhaps helping Mercury to meditate more easily. When there is an effort made to understand each other's differences, this is a very uplifting and inspirational configuration. It is good in fund raising or joint work for a charitable or religious organization, or perhaps a spiritual community, something they both truly "believe" in and wish to communicate to others.

MERCURY/PLUTO

Here we have a chance at psycho-drama in its prime. Mercury verbalizes Pluto's innermost feelings. This pair tends to have dialogues with each other that they wouldn't have with anyone else. Somehow the combination of these two stimulates thought on a very deep level of the subconscious, often bringing up deeply buried or long forgotten issues. There is a tendency for this interchange to be somewhat heavy with Pluto, while Mercury likes it light and carefree. They should be prepared for the depths of feeling they arouse in one another. The many close aspects of these two planets turning up quite frequently in married couples is understandable, as often one partner will bring up issues of another's past or childhood to help the other partner resolve and shed light upon those areas. This is an excellent therapist/client relationship as well as a pair involved in medical or biological research.

MERCURY/NODE

They are often on the same wavelength, and many married couples have this contact. The energy here stimulates people who want to share verbal exhanges at every level. This interaction emphasizes the need for open and honest communication. Mercury helps the Node with verbal and written expression. The Node usually is attracted to Mercury because of the learning that the Node receives - Mercury has information that the Node needs. The Node would give Mercury an audience or vehicle for expression, encouraging and promoting Mercury's ideas. The Mercury/South Node contact between two people can often suggest a replay of some past exchange that has taken place but was never quite completed. This will often concern Mercury's thinking or communication patterns. There is teaching and instruction taking place here as well.

MERCURY/ASCENDANT

The attraction occurs initially because the Ascendant is often attracted to Mercury's knowledge and ideas. Mer-

cury is a great sales person and the Ascendant is a ready
buyer. (If not ready, Mercury will talk the Ascendant into
it). The two may feel related, as if are were siblings, as
there is a tendency to act and think similarly. Additionally, Mercury inspires the Ascendant's thought processes
and they can achieve an excellent rapport in communications. Mercury may encourage the Ascendant to write or cat-
alogue all of their experiences. This influence is usually
strong as the Ascendant really respects Mercury's mental
processes. The Ascendant can usually identify with all the
things Mercury talks about. They would likely be a very
active pair, with interests in education and travel.

MERCURY/MIDHEAVEN

Many Mercury/MC aspects exist between married couples.
They have a lot to talk about with each other. They
identify with each other's thinking processes. Often they
work together or help organize each other in some specific
capacity. An excellent partnership would exist if the MC
hired Mercury as a sales representative, publicist. recep-
tionist or secretary. This can be an unusually good
business relationship where both people approach it in the
same manner and communicate freely and openly.

VENUS

"The first time ever I saw your face,
I thought the sun rose in your eyes
And the moon and the stars were the gifts you gave
To the dark and the end of the skies..."

Ewan MacColl
"The First Time Ever I Saw
Your Face"

RULER OF: TAURUS (2)   PRINCIPLE: Love, beauty,
           LIBRA (7)   affection, the feminine, art,
                               adoration, pleasure, social
                               interaction and values

WHAT IT REPRESENTS:

Traditionally, Venus embodies all that is feminine, all
that is beauty and all that is love. It has come to be
known as the archetype for woman, and in fact, the women's
movement uses the glyph for Venus as their logo. Yet,
regardless of gender, everyone has Venus in their chart.
Venus is the vehicle through which we express our love, our
likes and our ability to socially connect with our environment. A key factor in compatibility analysis, Venus
suggests the emphasis and boundaries we need to express our

77

love. Frequent Venus aspects among friends indicate the additional importance Venus plays in social interaction, along with our ability to harmonize with others. By sign, house and aspect, Venus represents our degree of capability to love one another and to love ourselves.

Because Venus still has rulership over two signs, Taurus and Libra, there are two areas assigned to Venus in the chart; very simply stated, they are love (Libra) and money (Taurus). The Venus association with money, values and possessions (the things Taurus represents) has to do with how we spend our money (what we value) rather than our capacity to earn money. Libra's influence on Venus shows how we choose to relate to the yin counterpart of ourselves and how we choose to join forces and share ourselves with another.

In relationships, the person whose Venus contacts our chart adds some form of love, beauty or pleasure to our lives. They usually make us feel good about ourselves or some aspect of our life. If the aspect is among lovers, they want to be involved in loving a great deal of the time; if among friends, they want to talk about love and share aspects of their love lives with each other quite a bit.

VENUS/VENUS

Here we have the mutual admiration society. A harmonious aspect between the two Venuses will definitely offset any otherwise unfriendly aspects in two charts. There is a feeling of comfort and ease when relating to one another. Both parties can find areas of compatibility quite easily, overlooking the not so agreeable parts. Usually there is a bond of togetherness involving a mutual interest or hobby. This may concern something in Venus's domain, such as beauty, attractiveness and the feminine concerns, or socializing with the same kind of people. They can share a lot about each other's love life together. The stressful aspects present not so much a challenge, but rather a look at the same issue from a different perspective. For instance, both love the same outfit or car, but totally disagree on the color or model. The challenge is to focus on similarities and to not be offended by differences.

VENUS/MARS

The highly touted aspect that everyone looks for in compatibility, Venus and Mars represent the archetypal feminine merging with the archetypal masculine. It is the ruler of Libra merging with the ruler of Aries, a natural polarity. With Venus representing the object of our desires and Mars representing our ability to go after what we desire, this can be a highly stimulating physical and emotional union. With Mars being a yang planet and Venus being a yin planet, the result is Mars usually taking the lead, with Venus accepting whatever is offered in its passive, receptive role (regardless of which gender has the Mars and which has the Venus). Yet they work this way, not in competition, but as if on cue, instinctively knowing their respective parts. Occasionally, Venus's gentle nature is slightly miffed by Mars's aggressiveness, but Venus works wonders on smoothing out all of Mars's rough areas. There is a desire for a particularly strong emphasis on romantic and sexual togetherness when Venus and Mars are prominent between two people.

VENUS/JUPITER

With this pair, both can inflate the areas in life that concern prosperity, gain, ease and comfort; in short, the finer pleasures of life. That includes whatever brings pleasure to each individual, whether on a material, mental or spiritual plane of understanding. It is no surprise that many married couples have this pair in close aspect to one another. An emphasis here is placed upon expanding one's horizons (traveling), one's social involvements (partying) and one's luxuries (spending). This aspect is also frequent among friends, as we choose our friends for joint pleasures, enjoying the process of giving and receiving. With this pair, it is likely Venus receiving and Jupiter giving, yet Venus gives much in love and admiration to boost Jupiter's ever-present sense of importance. They both have the tendency to overdo, so they could wind up so immersed in their one or two areas of pleasure that they totally ignore everything else. There can also be the danger of over-spending, over-exaggerating or over-indulging to the point of excessiveness. The overall feeling of these two being together promotes a sense of seeing life as a pleasure cruise or party, loving it all.

VENUS/SATURN

There is an attraction here based on the security and structure that Saturn can offer to Venus's need for those things, yet there seems to be a price to pay for this security. Venus, who is warm, often feels the shiver of Saturn's coolness. Venus may like frivolity and flirtatiousness and Saturn doesn't handle that too well. Venus likes to feel loved, appreciated and adored, and Saturn has a hard time expressing those feelings. Saturn is much better at offering security or dependability to a relationship than it is at being romantic or warm. In spite of this, there does exist a strong attraction between the two.

Venus offers warmth, beauty, sociability and often financial know-how to whomever it encounters. With Saturn's expertise at business and organization, they can often do very well together in a business setting.

Businesses that thrive with this combination include the artistic and deal with beauty or glamour in some way. They also share a love of the arts.

In many relationships that are not based on romantic intimacy and where it is not important to say "I love you" all the time, this pair does very well together. Venus adds sparkle to Saturn's way of doing business, and actually heightens and stimulates Saturn's sense of discipline.

VENUS/URANUS

There is a natural trine at work here, bringing in Venus's rulership over Libra and Uranus's rulership of Aquarius. Both planets have control of air signs which would heighten relationships with a high degree of mental stimulation. This aspect focuses the relationship on the ability to relate to each other and emphasize how the pair relates to friends and groups in general. There is a mutual interest here in exchanging ideas, inventions and perceptions, and reactions occur in a totally spontaneous way. They may have an extremely unique lifestyle or love life.

In stressful aspects, there is a tendency for Uranus, who is guided by spontaneous relationships, to explore, always noticing and socializing with others. Venus is looking for lasting love and doesn't like Uranus's "groupie" mannerisms. Therefore, the combination may find it difficult to live together for very long – Uranus needing freedom and room to breathe, while Venus is wanting closeness and attachment.

VENUS/NEPTUNE

This aspect is similar to Moon/Neptune, although with Venus/Neptune, the attraction is often the love at first sight kind. There is a significant occurrence of this pair in couples who are attracted romantically to one another. It's very easy to "become one with" each other in this situation. This yin pair deals with glamour, sensitivity and has an acute ability to manifest creative, artistic and mediumistic channels of awareness into physical form.

In stressful aspects between these planets, there are unspoken or undefined problems. As time goes on, one of the partners feels there is something underlying this relationship that is preventing it from ever being fully consummated. The fear on the part of Neptune to become totally involved always seems to creep in, but the attraction towards Venus is so powerful that Neptune can't fully release the relationship either. Where good, old-fashioned romantic love is important (candlelight, wine, nice music, etc.), this pair is tops.

VENUS/PLUTO

A polarity pair working together here brings in Venus's rulership over Taurus and Pluto's over Scorpio. An emphasis exists on sharing resources, wealth and love – in short, whatever one has becomes the other's (in most cases). The relationship will naturally and easily enjoy a focus on sexual intimacy when they are closely aspected.

Venus helps Pluto become less possessive, especially materially, except for one area: letting go of Venus itself. This can be an extremely possessive relationship when it comes to love, and this aspect shows up frequently in the charts of marrieds and lovers. One will occassionally share wealth or good fortune with others, but rarely if ever, a lover or a mate. Even among friends who are not lovers, this aspect seems to invite jealousy or possessiveness in third party encounters. The message this aspect sends is to be careful when Venus's flirtatious nature sets Pluto's atomic reactors in motion, or when Pluto's frequent expression of raw sensuality causes Venus's attachment-oriented nature to feel threatened. Among lovers, there is a focus on sexual intimacy, and among friends, much conversation about it. Like Moon/Pluto, the people with strong Venus/Pluto contacts experience a healthy, enjoyable sex life with one another.

VENUS/NODE

A positive flow of energy exists here, as both deal with people and their social calendar quite a bit. Venus already moves in the circles the Node is trying to reach, and in social settings, this is a plus. There is also the tendency to search out the areas in each other that they both enjoy and overlook the unpleasantries. In friends, Venus often opens up feminine and artistic channels to the Node. In lovers, the Venus/South Node conjunction will often reveal old love affairs. South Node experiences an acute receptivity to Venus where love and romance are concerned.

VENUS/ASCENDANT

This combination suggests that with the Ascendant, there is a personal identity with and desire to become a part of Venus's love. Venus would make the Ascendant feel more attractive and desirable, bringing out its nicer qualities. The Ascendant responds by just feeling good around Venus. This relationship is excellent for two people working together or involved in fashion, beauty and the arts. They have an innate ability to soothe and comfort each other.

VENUS/MIDHEAVEN

Venus flatters and stimulates the Midheaven's sense of accomplishment and ambition, so typically one is attracted to (Venus) what someone else is already achieving (MC). Venus often brings beauty and/or love to this relationship while the Midheaven offers position and/or status. This pair would be a friendly union and usually serves to heighten or broaden one's social circle, one's sense of accomplishment in the world or one's sense of what they really enjoy out of life and feel is important. It is also an excellent aspect for working together in businesses involving the arts, fashion, femininity and any consumer products that would serve women.

MARS

"Let's get physical, physical,
I wanna get physical
Let's get into physical,
Let me hear your body talk..."

Stephen A. Kipner & Terry
Shaddick
"Physical"

RULER OF: ARIES (1)   PRINCIPLE: energy, enthusiasm
                              self motivation, libido,
                              physical action, animus,
                              aggressiveness, anger

WHAT IT REPRESENTS:

Mars is the planet that represents energy level in its purest form: how much energy we have and how we expend it. It represents our desire to go after what we really want in life. For this reason, I primarily choose Mars as a vocational indicator. We are much happier in jobs or professions we desire, have the energy to do and at which we are good. As ruler of Aries, a sign representing the self, Mars tends to act in a "me first" manner, again emphasizing personal needs, passions and drives. It also has a child-like quality (as ruler of Aries) and can often express itself as immaturity and impatience.

In a relationship, the Mars placement is important because the Mars energy needs to be well balanced with the partner in order to interrelate effectively. Mars can be warm-hearted or hot-headed. Those with heavily stressed Mars charts may find it difficult to stay in a relationship very long because of a lack of consideration, inability to compromise and frequent flare-ups or temper tantrums. A well-integrated Mars heightens and stimulates the amount of work that is accomplished and arouses the desires and sexual needs of each other. In almost every case of relationships analyzed, the Mars of one chart was in active contact with a yin planet in the other, creating a natural polarity.

MARS/MARS

Fire meets fire - a highly emotional aspect that can arouse passion or anger. Aspects between two Marses should be relatively stress-free to ensure a non-violent and/or non-argumentative relationship. A Mars/Mars conjunction between two people can stimulate friendship, but it might be a competitive type of friendship.

The trine or sextile series usually produces a stimulating and active relationship wherein each party enjoys spending time with the other, emphasizing enthusiasm and action in their relationship. They would have similar energy levels, waking and sleeping habits and bodily rhythms. They put out equal amounts of energy in any given area. The square series may be very difficult to handle because both parties try to lead and direct the other.

MARS/JUPITER

Both yang, fiery planets have the shared characteristics of thinking and acting in a BIG way (expressing ego), and putting much of their energy into the same kinds of activities. Mars is always ready with new ideas and projects, while Jupiter exaggerates their importance, so pretty soon, what started out as a part-time hobby becomes an all-consuming issue involving 10 other people and every dollar that can be acquired. Fortunately, this combination can produce a quick burn-out, so this all-consuming passion does not last forever. This team would work well in sales and promotion, working for the same corporation or enterprise. They would also do well in sales groups that deal with motivational selling. Any venture requiring a good deal of drama and flair would be a likely area for these two. It is most definitely a positive thinking, prosperity-conscious attitude that would develop from the association of these two planets.

MARS/SATURN

There is a strong attraction at work between these two planets, although sometimes it can be considered a problem. Mars (yang) is great at playing offense while Saturn (yin) prefers defense. Thus, in many instances they function better as a team than in individual combat. In a one-to-one relationship, they press each other's buttons and react accordingly. Mars comes out with it and Saturn represses it, so in some cases, Mars's fire gets put out by Saturn's restrictiveness. Mars will see Saturn as somewhat stuffy, old-fashioned and slow moving, whereas Saturn views Mars as raucous, headstrong and rebellious. Yet in team-work, they will defend each other staunchly when dealing with the outside world. Mars has something to learn from Saturn or they would not be together in the first place. Mars often attracts Saturn or Saturn types to help anchor and focus the sometimes wild and rebellious activity of Mars, but can also resent Saturn's disciplinarian behavior, interpreting it as "someone who's always trying to prevent me from doing what I want to do." They do provide what each one lacks, however, so it can be a very useful relationship. The conjunction occurs more often between business associates, family and friends than in couples who are romantically involved.

MARS/URANUS

The natural rulers of Aries and Aquarius combine here to produce a highly active mental force of original, independent and innovative thought. They bounce creative ideas back and forth and need a stimulating outlet for each other's high adrenaline producing energies. This is a good combination for pairs involved in the same kind of work and interests, including astrology, computer sciences, video and electronics or any high-tech area. Uranus creates a strong mental outlet for Mars and this combination would lean towards brilliance or genius in some area. Both must be allowed maximum freedom of thought and expression, with few restrictions placed on the relationship for best results.

MARS/NEPTUNE

The polarity between an active Mars (+) and a receptive Neptune (-) indicates a very different set of natural energies coming together that should hopefully complement each other. This is the Aries ruler (Mars) meeting the Pisces ruler (Neptune). The positive expression of this configuration is strong self identification with and stimulation (Mars) of the partner's ideals, dreams and fantasies (Neptune). Pyschic (Neptune) energy (Mars) can be highly stimulated between one another. The positive focus would be for Neptune to help Mars understand the importance of reflection, meditation, quiet, creative fantasy and artistic pursuits, while Mars helps energize Neptune and get moving on those ideas.

The negative manifestation is Neptune's tendency to create a real drain on Mars's vital energies and desires, resulting in feelings of inadequacy, fatigue and sometimes frigidity or impotence. If Mars if weakened or easily influenced, Neptune will focus this relationship on fantasy, illusion and lethargy. Neptune often forces guilt as an issue, which Mars handles poorly. Neptune may be lost in fantasy, sleep or addictive tendencies, while Mars prefers to be active, stimulated and energized. There is a high degree of sexual arousal between this pair.

MARS/PLUTO

These two planets can create a compulsive, animal magnetism between each other. The contacts between this pair show up frequently in many love relationships, indicating a strong intimate physical and emotional involvement. Both planets share rulership of Aries and Scorpio, and there is an emphasis on personal desires, sexual intimacy and deep passion. A powerfully transforming sexual energy exists between the two. Mars can act out Pluto's innermost desires and cravings, often in a way that is threatening to Pluto. Pluto likes secrets and certain things kept undercover, so Mars's playfulness with these protective areas will sometimes leave Pluto feeling dangerously exposed, embarrassed and vulnerable. However, similar to the Venus/Pluto configuration, here there are deep, profound feelings aroused between this pair. The bond can hardly be broken through one or two misunderstandings. There also tends to be jealousy or possessiveness because the bond is so strong and the need so great. In aspects that present real challenge to one another, be careful of abusive tendencies that can surface.

MARS/NODE

These two usually admire many things about each other. The Node often acts as a guide (teacher, parent, etc.) for Mars or sets the example that Mars chooses to emulate. The Node is drawn to Mars's unique ability to be oneself - a natural, spontaneous mannerism. They often have the same physical interests or are attracted to each other physically. A stressful contact can produce the attitude that "Mars is just too immature" and "The Node always tries to run my life." The South Node can be very sensitive to Mars's aggressive energy, and can sometimes be a victim of Mars's hostility, anger or abuse.

MARS/ASCENDANT

Personal identification between these two is quite strong, for Mars rules the natural First House and Ascendant. With the conjunction, they tend to bring out the childlike qualities in each other, wanting to play, romp and have lots of fun. They spend hours talking, enjoy the same pleasures and have similar drives and work-related interests. Mars tends to have a higher energy level or sex drive and will usually be the pusher, prodding the Ascendant to get motivated or moving in a certain area. If the aspect is not a relaxed one between the two, it could create resentment or resistance from the Ascendant. For instance, when Mars is in tense aspect to the other's Ascendant, the Ascendant can feel threatened or bullied by Mars. There is a slight danger of competition and problems could occur in situations in which they are competing for the same job or the affections of someone they both admire. In a love relationship, the sexual contact and physical drives are strong and there exists a nice attraction.

MARS/MIDHEAVEN

A high percentage of couples who live together have connecting aspects between one's Mars and the other's Midheaven. A dynamic interplay exists here with the Mars fire fueling the MC's ambitions and direction. They may be drawn together at a time in their life when they are striving to achieve the same goals and are attracted to the same kinds of people. Similar to Mars/Node, Mars/Midheaven can often play out a parent-child role with each other that also involves professional goals.

This aspect often brings family situations that challenge Mars's assertiveness and test Mars's endurance. Mars has the ability and energy to motivate the MC. In a tense aspect, this will be experienced as uncomfortable for the MC who wishes Mars would slow down, exhibit more patience and stop instigating all of the time.

JUPITER

"He had white horses and ladies by the score,
All dressed in satin and waiting by the door,
Oh, what a lucky man he was..."

Greg Lake
"Lucky Man"

RULER OF: SAGITTARIUS (9)   PRINCIPLE: Expansion, travel, abundance, the future, law, philosophy, education, the good life

WHAT IT REPRESENTS:

Jupiter, the largest physical planet in our solar system, represents that part of our life where we tend to get the most satisfaction, or at least look for the most satisfaction. We tend to emphasize and expand the principles of the sign and house Jupiter occupies, as if the sky was the limit and no amount of reason or caution will do. We go for it with a belief that success will be ours - and it usually is, because we believe it. Strong Jupiter types will usually "raise the spirits" of others. Raising the spirits can include whatever that takes, including raising the bottle.

Jupiter seeks to expand in every area and whether this expansion is in materialistic areas, emotional cravings or philosohical pursuits, chances are that Jupiter contacts with another will expand you in some way. It is a planet of wealth or gain, and wealth can be expressed through spiritual and philosophical abundance as well. Most of the Jupiter contacts that occur between two people involve the Jupiter person giving help, financial aid, business advice, friendship or advancement of some kind to the other.

The action we take to expand our role in society is also a function of Jupiter, because it combines the social urges we have with the purpose we seek to be helpful or useful. In this way, most Jupiter contacts will expand our awareness of social obligations and create a useful and pleasurable outlet. Jupiter stays in a sign approximately one year, circling the entire zodiac in 12 years. This corresponds to the Chinese zodiac, each sign appearing once every 12 years.

JUPITER/JUPITER

A close Jupiter/Jupiter contact will automatically bring respect, sharing and creative purpose to a relationship. Most often, philosophies and outlooks on life are similar, and both people admire each other's role in the community or extended family. Quite often, Jupiters are conjunct by sign in people who choose to work together in community affairs, teaching or public relations. Jupiter returns to the same sign every 12 years, and whether the age gap is 12, 24, 36 or 48 years, many close friendships develop between these people, because Jupiter occupies the same sign. They can have the utmost respect and trust for each other. In their relationship, they tend to want "the best of everything." The only drawback with a close Jupiter aspect can be the exaggeration or over-indulgence that is so common with Jupiter.

JUPITER/SATURN

Jupiter and Saturn are the two giants of our solar system and rule the signs and houses of the astrological wheel that point straight up, towards which we are all reaching. As planetary rulers, they represent the top - materially and spiritually. Though what they are striving for is different, they are both striving and can serve to complement each other well. For instance, Jupiter deals with how we can expand our interests in the community and what benefits come from that process, while Saturn seems to deal with the duties, responsibilities and demands society asks of us. Accordingly, in a couple, Jupiter can be the optimistic partner while Saturn takes the pessimistic view. Jupiter may want to spend, while Saturn wants to control the budget. Jupiter loves over-indulgence, richness, flamboyance

and has a liberal attitude. Saturn prefers discipline, dis-
cretion and conservative attitudes. Couples who have these
planets in strong aspect are somehow keeping each other in
check and balance, although Saturn may see Jupiter as too
indulgent, while Jupiter may view Saturn as too conservative. They may do better in a business setting than in a
living situation. Perhaps the company treasurer should
have a strong Saturn contact with the company's Jupiter to
control company spending.

JUPITER/URANUS

This couple is expanded through learning, teaching and
scientific channels of awareness and seems to enhance free-
spirited, open communications between two people. They
have a natural kind of friendliness with each other, being
rulers of Sagittarius and Aquarius respectively. One would
expect a couple with this aspect prominent to be pace set-
ters, risk-takers and adventurers with high priorities for
education, intellectual, scientific and philosophical development. Astrology, technology, computers and engineering
could be a common ground for many with this aspect.
Because Jupiter is mutable in nature and Uranus is fixed,
problems that might arise from this pair can be situations
where Uranus is not being open enough to change or flexible
enough in viewpoint for Jupiter's broad spectrum and high
spirited nature. Yet, Uranus does desire freedom and room
to breathe, so the combination produces a great deal of
wanderlust, whether physical or mental.

JUPITER/NEPTUNE

The aspects between these two planets is high among
couples. Jupiter's expansiveness connects to the sensitive
nature of Neptune to create a union based on shared philosophies, feelings and ways of expressing their beliefs and
religious/spiritual attitudes. In fact, much of their relationship may revolve around their spiritual attitudes and
beliefs, their search to fulfill some high ideal. There
can be much idealism in this combination as both planets co-
rule Pisces. Jupiter, a yang planet, is a great deal more
outgoing and assertive than Neptune, a yin planet, but the
pair seems balanced and especially sympathetic to one another. Jupiter is undoubtedly the more outspoken of the two,
as is the Sagittarian tendency Any problems experienced
can or may be attributed to Neptune's silent resistance
toward Jupiter's flamboyance. They are both prone to
escape through indulgence and with their shared interest in
unhealthy addictions, this could be a problem if they
allowed it to get out of hand or live in their illusions.
Still, there is a strong psychic bond, and most of all,
trust and respect for one another.

JUPITER/PLUTO

There is almost no boundary or limit to discussions between these two. They both think in terms of the infinite, and whether that concept is channeled into discussion or actual achievement, it is a powerful planetary pair at work. This pair has been referred to as the "once in a lifetime chance" or a "one in a million shot." Ebertin refers to this midpoint combination as "The desire for power (plutocracy)" (The Combination of Stellar Influences, p. 176). In stressful aspects between these two, there can be a fight for control of each other in a most negative way. Jupiter is typically giving in nature and Pluto knows best how to use or take. Resentment can build if they aren't cautious of this situation. With Jupiter's quest for knowledge and Pluto's probe fo the mysterious, this team together needs to understand everything. Be careful, though, because what Jupiter says in jest, Pluto can take all too seriously. Overall, this pair should enjoy the emotional, philosophical and spiritual stimulation that each induces in the other.

JUPITER/NODE

The North Node is sometimes referred to as another version of Jupiter, so there is an attraction based on similarity. They are both goal-oriented toward expanding their joint energies and building something BIG together. They are generally proud of each other and promote one another. Because the nodal contacts imply a karmic pattern and Jupiter an embodiment of philosophies, this pair has a leaning towards philosophical issues in their relationship together. They may have been brought together through their similar philosophical orientation. With the Jupiter/South Node conjunction, the South Node is the receiver for what Jupiter has to give.

JUPITER/ASCENDANT

Jupiter's role as giver or promoter finds a nice avenue of expression with the Ascendant, because it is the most personal point in a chart. The Ascendant looks up to and respects Jupiter, and Jupiter brings qualities to the Ascendant that say, "Here I am and here is what I have to offer. It's yours for the asking." The two are tied closely together in charts of people choosing to live their lives together. Long-time friends and business partners find Jupiter/Ascendant contacts important, because of the importance, respect and kindness these two often bring out in each other.

JUPITER/MIDHEAVEN

The Midheaven is another vehicle through which Jupiter can advertise, promote and endorse. With the Midheaven, however, we may be referring more to family ties or professional associations, as the Midheaven tends to be what we are reaching for, based on society or family programming. Ebertin calls this pair "the consciousness of aim or objective in life" (ibid, p. 182), so they will be working on joint goals and objectives together. Nevertheless, the union here should produce few obstacles, if any, as they both are "climbing."

SATURN

"Desperado, why don't you come to your senses
Come down from your fences, open the gate.
It may be raining, but there's a rainbow above you.
You better let somebody love you before it's
too late..."

Don Henley & Glenn Frey
"Desperado"

RULER OF: **CAPRICORN (10)**   **PRINCIPLE:** form, discipline,
           AQUARIUS (11)   responsibility, structure,
                                        age, endurance, authority,
                                        law, time

WHAT IT REPRESENTS:

The multi-ringed planet Saturn, long feared and awed, is one of the keys to life on earth. The more we discover of its rings, the more layers we unlock to the mysteries of life. Saturn is the bringer of form, discipline, challenge and law. Saturn, many times, is they key in our charts to our own weakness or vulnerability and gives us many chances to deal with them through its transits. Above all else, Saturn is form. In Capricorn, it is CON-form. In Aquarius, it is RE-form.

In relationships, Saturn's exaltation (a term meaning high honors bestowed) occurs in Libra the scales, the sign of partnerships, balance and equality. To understand Saturn, you must be on an equal par with another. You must learn to take and learn to give. You must learn to serve before you can be served.

Because Saturn is taken so seriously by most of us and we are working so hard to integrate its function properly, it may be too much of a challenge in relationships with others. It may be where we expect others to be perfect, and because they never are, it can become a vulnerable area. Saturn likes the role of parent or teacher and Saturn contacts with another's chart show seriousness and responsi-

bility.   Saturn does things by the book. It is more willing
to marry when it is time to marry than to live out of
wedlock, because marriage is the proper thing to do.
Saturn says, "I will take care of you and I'll support you –
morally, financially, emotionally, etc. But these are the
rules you to which you must adhere. If you can't follow
these rules, we'll divorce," (also by the book).

Although Saturn contacts may be the binding factor at
the onset of a relationship, it may ultimately represent
the pressure that causes a breakup as well. The Saturn of
one partner contacting the Sun of the other appeared in a
fairly high percentage of marriages. Saturn holds a lot of
aspects to Mars in both business relationships and marriage
and to Mercury in both business relationships and friendships.   Saturn makes many aspects to both Venus and the
Moon in many relationships, however, most of those relationships are either dissolved or divorced. The sensitive Moon
and loving Venus, it seems, cannot take the seriousness and
apparent inhibitions of Saturn.   Saturn contacts to the
angles, Ascendant, Midheaven, Vertex and East Point, occur
in a very high percentage of couples, although not necessarily in couples that stay together forever. It might be
deduced from this that any important relationship of one's
life will have one person's Saturn contacting the angles or
the personal planets of the other.

An important consideration to think about regarding
Saturn's relationship to Jupiter and the outer planets is
that all of these planets (Jupiter, Saturn, Uranus, Neptune
and Pluto) were mythological lords of their particular domain (Zeus, Chronos, Ouranos, Poseidon and Hades respectively) and held much power at one time or another. For this
reason, they demand and deserve a certain respect for their
position.   When not given this respect for their particular
expertise or when their territorial rights are not observed, there are often power struggles that result. Therefore, close contacts of these planets to another's outer
planets may serve to remind us of that. Saturn, particularly, is politically minded and plays by the rules. Saturn's
position in a horoscope and its position in relationship to
someone else's horoscope, suggests that authority and age
be respected and acknowledged. This is particularly
troublesome when there is a parent/child or employer/
employee relationship that involves these points.

SATURN/SATURN

Many couples of the same age have the Saturn/Saturn
conjunction because it stays in a sign approximately 2-1/2
years.   It squares itself every 7 years. Relationships
that have Saturn square (7 years apart) or in opposition
(14 years apart) seem to have a great deal of attraction to
each other, albeit a struggle.   Of course, many parent/
child pairs have the conjunction of their Saturns, because
the Saturn return period (age 28-30) is a very popular
child-bearing period.   The close Saturn to Saturn contact

in a partnership often plays out a missing parent role. Depending on how each person handles his own Saturn, the other's Saturn will represent limits and law and will make binding restrictions in many ways. Yet, many who lack self-discipline feel they need to have these limits set upon them. Whatever the combination, if the Saturns are close, they will usually wind up playing out the parent-child role for each other, and may alternate who plays which role from time to time.

SATURN/URANUS

Here is where the God of Conform meets the God of Reform. Mythologically, this was a father-son relationship that told of Uranus the father swallowing all of his children until crafty Saturn came along, castrated father Uranus and promptly put an end to that problem. Thus, what we are seeing here is the potential for creative ideas (offspring) to be severely suppressed (swallowed up) until they finally are completely aborted. This may give some clues to the Saturn/Uranus relationship when they are not tuning into one another and respecting each other's natural laws. This is, of course, not intentionally done or consciously expressed between the two people who find themselves attracted to one another with this configuration, just as it isn't in an individual's natal chart who has these demanding gods in high focus. Yet it is something one must be acutely aware of in attempting to successfully integrate these two energies.
Because these two planets' energies represent such diverse principles, a harmonious contact between the two should at least offer more support for each other's differences than a tension aspect, which will often cause the roof to shake. There is nervous tension and irritability with Uranus, and often a slow, cautious, earthbound resistance displayed by Saturn. When this is the case and there does not seem to be willingness on the part of either to give up the struggle, there may be trouble. Ultimately, the person in this relationship embodied by Saturn is being presented with opportunities to look at new ways of doing things, at accepting change as the only constant and at letting the past make way for the future. Uranus, then, is learning that creative, electrical sparks of genius are only useful to humanity if they are grounded in some form.

SATURN/NEPTUNE

These are two yin planets, the ruler of Capricorn (the earth) and Pisces (the sea) respectively. Saturn is very much concerned with the physical form and material responsibility, while Neptune prefers traveling to the inner planes through a creative, meditative or spiritual journey. On a positive plane of expression, Saturn gives form and substance to Neptune's creative visualization and imagery process, whereas Neptune can inspire Saturn to fulfill his dreams, to step out of his world of fact and into creative fantasy or imagery on occasion.

Depression can be common for both of these planets, so care is needed to avoid emphasizing any negativity in the relationship. There can be a deep sense of isolation and responsibility towards each other. Saturn emphasizes achievement, urging Neptune to get out of his fantasy world and back to work. Neptune's response may be to drown himself in his sorrows or escape even further from reality through his favorite addictions, whether they be drugs and alcohol or sleep. Both, however, share a sensitivity, and while Saturn is somewhat reserved in expressing that sensitivity, Neptune can sense it acutely. They have a tendency to have a deeply felt exchange on a non-verbal level.

SATURN/PLUTO

The rulers of Capricorn and Scorpio form a natural sextile to each other, so they do have the opportunity for peaceful coexistence. Yet both are power seekers, manifesting a deep need from within (Pluto) to actualize one's ability in a responsible (Saturn) way. Saturn presents Pluto with the challenge of rebuilding and reworking all the areas Pluto has torn down. Their best role together is to work on personal reform, but if that is too threatening and their walls are too thick, they can always channel the energy into something less personal but still important - social and governmental reforms, for instance. This is one of the best and most creative uses of these two energies when working together.

They both need to be "in charge." In the more tense aspects, Pluto seeks to demolish the old to make way for the new, but Saturn doesn't break down easily. The ensuing struggle may be slow, painful and laborious. When working against each other, it can become a very difficult, no-win situation. They will both have "met their match," and hopefully combined their powerful ability to leave a legacy that future generations can appreciate.

SATURN/NODE

Saturn and the North Node both represent karmic areas of responsibility. Saturn helps strengthen our physical reality by pointing out areas of needed discipline. The Nodes show us experiences our soul needs for growth and progress. Thus, the frequent contact between these two in marriage charts suggests a willingness to assist each other's progress. Saturn rules Capricorn and the North Node has an affinity with the MC (see the section on the Nodes), thus, an association between these two suggests the path is ultimately the same. There is usually a great deal of care, protection and parenting here, as the Node responds to Saturn's teachings. I've also seen this aspect occur between family members who have expressed some hardships in dealing with each other.

In the Saturn/South Node conjunction, more hardship has been observed. The South Node will be drawn to Saturn, but also will be intimidated by Saturn's attitude of taking itself so seriously. The South Node sees through Saturn's vulnerabilities, but Saturn is typically too restrained and quite resistant to the South Node's suggestions for change. Saturn likes to have control. South Node is all too aware of the discomfort this relationship may be causing, but often feels that circumstances (karma?) are forcing them together to work it out. Perhaps there is a karmic debt being paid here - and Saturn seems to be the one who is collecting the bill. The Saturn/Node contact (North or South) is one that shows up quite frequently among business partnerships.

SATURN/ASCENDANT

The Saturn of one chart contacts the Ascendant/ Descendant axis of the other chart quite frequently in long term relationships. This is another parent/child role being played out, with the Ascendant (Aries undertones) taking on the role of child and Saturn (Capricorn ruler) being the dutiful parent, teacher. guide and so forth. Obviously the Ascendant has a personal identification with and a need for a structuring agent in its life or it would not have attracted Saturn in the first place. The Ascendant is pulling in Saturn's abilities at parenting, protectiveness, responsibility and care which Saturn is so good at giving. The main restriction here would come when the child (Ascendant) goes through its periods of rebellion against authority and seeks to be independent, while Saturn sits waiting for the phase to pass. The Ascendant (child), however, can give Saturn some room to play, loosen up and be a child, if Saturn is willing to let its walls down long enough to let that happen.

SATURN/MIDHEAVEN

In many cases, Saturn falls on the Midheaven of those who work together and in the 4th House of those who live together. This is no real surprise because Saturn can teach, discipline and organize the MC's goals and role in the public while working together, and offer parental guidance and security to those with whom he lives.

Security is a reason many people stay with their mate, even though there is little or no romance left in the relationship. When they are talking of security, they are speaking of Saturn. Saturn contacts in long term marriages appear to be quite numerous. Saturn may help to organize and structure the MC's long term goals, while the MC may give Saturn an outlet for his work energy. Let's not forget that Saturn is the natural ruler of the 10th House and the MC is the 10th House doorway, so they have quite a strong resemblance to one another.

The Saturn/MC relationship also involves both people's role and status in society, so the attraction may be based on one or both acknowledging that each is good for the other's reputation and status. In other words, parents and bosses would likely feel this person is "good for you." People who come together with this aspect may have an inbred need for that kind of approval in their relationship.

URANUS

"Now here you go again, you say you want your freedom
Well, who am I to keep you down
It's only right that you should play the way you
Feel it, but listen carefully to the sound
Of your loneliness..."

Stevie Nicks
"Dreams"

RULER OF: AQUARIUS (11)

PRINCIPLE: the awakener, reformer, catalyst for change, freedom-seeker, innovative, magnetic and electrical impulses to the brain

WHAT IT REPRESENTS:

As the higher octave of Mercury, Uranus represents a different kind of mental and communicative energy - one involving electrical impulses that occur quite suddenly. Among people whose higher frequencies are open and receptive, this registers as creative intelligence or telepathy. Among those whose higher frequencies are blocked, the waves become scrambled and the result can be feelings of hypertension, craziness or insanity. Uranus operates with lightning speed and its sudden bolts of energy impact us in the same way. It seeks to awaken, reform, catalyze and change whatever is in its path with a magnetism that is hard to ignore. A high mental stimulation is aroused when within the aura of Uranus.

Uranus has an 84-year cycle around the zodiac, changing signs every seven years, thus the seven-year itch to break out of a routine and declare freedom. Halfway through its cycle, anywhere from age 38 to 42 years, this freedom seeking phase is particularly strong, as the opposition of Uranus to its natal position is being experienced, prompting each of us to get in touch with areas of life that need reform. Of course, people with an active Uranus to begin with seem to go through this process on a continual basis throughout their lives. Whether the changes are made physically or in attitude, the results are usually that this redirection results in more meaningful activity for the individual.

In relationships that feature strong Uranus ties, there is a magnetic energy that is usually felt immediately. The person you are meeting is bringing Uranus to you in some way. Thus, there is a magnetism that is hard to define. If your blood starts rushing wildly, your palms are becoming sweaty and you are experiencing an overwhelming reaction drawing you into their aura, no doubt you have just been struck by a thunderbolt called Uranus.

Uranus seems prominent in every case of sudden attraction, unusual meetings and highly nervous, anxious interchanges that take place between two people. Uranus makes strong contacts to both the Sun and the Moon of another individual in cases of marriage and divorce. Long thought to be the planet of divorce, Uranus merely seeks to awaken one to adopt new attitudes and lifestyles. If the marriage or relationship cannot keep up with those changes, then yes, it spells divorce. But in more cases than not, it is merely asking for progress, innovation and upliftment. When both people are involved in this process, there is no reason for a break-up. Uranus both sends and receives high energy stimulation and this is usually the first thing experienced when a Uranus contact is strong between two people.

URANUS/URANUS

A highly active arousal and stimulation of each other will occur when the Uranus of one person contacts the Uranus of the other. The conjunction occurs quite frequently between two people in married relationships as it stays in a sign seven years. When the aspect is extremely close (within 1 degree), the two people may feel the air charged with electrical currents; they will seem to be able to register each other's thoughtwaves in a very natural manner, as if they were their own. The square of Uranus between two people will occur when there is a 21 year age difference, which is more common in a parent/child relationship. The square is more difficult to deal with as the changes each seeks to make are often explosive and at cross-purposes to each other's natural inclinations. The parent whose Uranus squares, inconjuncts or opposes the child's will have a difficult time in the same household unless they allow a lot of room for growth. Without a doubt, they will be instrumental in breaking each other of habit patterns and routines in need of change. When the parent asserts independence, the child rebels; when the child tries to assert his independence, the parent reacts. A close contact between the two Uranuses, however, will at least keep the relationship from getting dull.

URANUS/NEPTUNE

The God of the airwaves meets the God of the waterways.
A strong aspect between these two planets produces a highly
stimulating (Uranus) psychic sensitivity (Neptune) in each
other. Both of these planets are transcendental in nature,
and an aspect between the two would suggest a powerful
force at work. They are both planets that represent the
energy of the collective unconscious, but they work in different ways. Although they possess a heightened awareness
and sensitivity between them, Uranus is more excitable,
electrical and spontaneous, whereas Neptune is mellower and
slower to react. In married couples, the square and the
opposition occur frequently, creating a polarity effect.

The challenge this aspect brings involves a difference
in rhythm and can be just what the other needs. Uranus is
the stimulant and Neptune is the tranquilizer in most situations. Because Uranus types are on a natural "high" with
highly charged nervous systems, they do not need artificial
stimulants in their system. These things (caffeine, for
example) have ten times the affect on them as they do on
others. They require calming, tranquil, soothing remedies
such as herbal teas, or the kind of soothing that Neptune
types are so good at giving. Neptune, on the other hand,
already tranquil and calm, can use the stimulation and fast
paced, electrical charges that Uranus's energy can provide
for them.

URANUS/PLUTO

The last conjunction of these two planets took place
between 1963 and 1967 and best describes the massive
rebellion and change that was the keynote of the tumultuous
1960's. Uranus's keynote is revolution and change, whereas
Pluto's realm is death, rebirth and regeneration. The
combined energies of these two planets seem to signal times
of great change and manifest these changes in an often
devastating manner.

In a person's chart, this conjunction produces highly
reactive energy patterns from within that demand an immediate outlet. If not properly channeled, it can manifest in
personal chaos and destructiveness. When two people come
together with a strong Uranus/Pluto contact, they will feel
as if they were drawn together by forces greater than
either of them and will tend to promote each other in areas
where personal changes need to be made. In fact, they may
meet at a time when both are seeking to make great changes
in their personal lives, at a time when both are in a
growth process. Pluto may force Uranus into a more struc-
tured mode, whereas Uranus forces Pluto to open up to new
ways of expressing what is deeply rooted within the psyche.
Many children born in the 1940's and 1950's have Uranus on
their parents' Plutos. This aspect has been instrumental
in awakening what has been deeply rooted in the parents'
psyches symbolized by Pluto's position in the horoscope.

URANUS/NODE

Uranus will usually have a sudden flash of deja vu when encountering the Node. Uranus may not be aware of the nature of the relationship, but will certainly recognize a familiarity of some kind. The Node will see Uranus as a chance to break away from dependencies, habits and routines while Uranus promotes the progressive, unusual and avant-garde. Uranus also offers a sort of genius or brilliance that dazzles the Node. The South Node is also quite attracted by Uranus and will usually have a strong friendship or relationship with Uranus that is quite intense. Uranus/Nodal contacts are prominent in all kinds of stimulating relationships. Although attracted by Uranus's independent nature and casual manner, both Nodes will be somewhat threatened by it, as constant change offers very little of the type of security and stability with which the Nodes are comfortable.

URANUS/ASCENDANT

The highly charismatic energy exchange is here, but so is the unpredictability of the relationship. The personal identity of the Ascendant relates to and is stimulated by Uranus's power of attraction. This can be a broadening experience for both parties, as Uranus gets a closer look at his erratic energy patterns through the Ascendant, while the Ascendant is stimulated and magnetized by Uranus. As natural rulers of Aquarius and the 1st House respectively, this is a relationship intent on promoting the unique, getting involved in the same interests and getting used to the concept that the only thing certain is change. The thing to remember here, as is the case typically with Uranus, is that Uranus doesn't want to feel possessed, tied down or inhibited in any way. Aspects to the Ascendant /Descendant axis will be a strong, magnetic association, and show up frequently among couples. The only warning here is for the Ascendant to try not to control or make demands or expectations of Uranus - that will send Uranus running.

URANUS/MIDHEAVEN

This pair works similarly to Uranus/Ascendant, showing up strongly in all kinds of relationships, except that this one dominates business relationships. Arenas where these two showed strongly seemed to be in Uranus types of professions or interests - computers, video games, astrology, science or engineering, and in close friends that have these interests in common.

They both seem to have uncommon qualities that attract them to each other and cause them to stand out in a crowd because of their uniqueness. Often the difference is noticeable - a great age gap, racial gap or gender similarity.

It may be a relationship whose only concern is with their one common bond of interest, having very little to do with each other in other areas. The unpredictible urges of Uranus would suggest that they would give each other a lot of room within the relationship to do other things, but that in their areas of shared interest, the contact is fast moving and intense.

NEPTUNE

"What a fool believes, he sees
No wise man has the power to reason away
What seems to be
Is always better than nothing
And nothing at all..."

Ken Loggins & Michael McDonald
"What a Fool Believes"

RULER OF: PISCES (12)

PRINCIPLE: imaginative, illusive, mystical, creative, psychic or other worldly, confusing, deceptive or addictive

WHAT IT REPRESENTS:

Most of us will only experience half of Neptune's 165 year cycle around the zodiac in one lifetime. Therefore, the slow-moving but subtle effects it has upon us when transiting planets in our chart should not be underestimated, like all the outer planets' transits. For many, Neptune is hard to put a finger on and capture. As soon as you think you have Neptune all figured out, it seems to disappear in a magic puff of smoke and you find yourself rubbing your eyes, wondering if you really saw it at all. Perhaps this is because what Neptune represents is intangible, like air itself. It is real, but how do you draw a picture of it or describe it to someone else?

Perhaps more than anything else, Neptune governs vision, but not vision with the physical eyes. With those eyes, it's quite out of focus. The vision Neptune governs is the third eye, or what is scientifically referred to as the pineal gland in the center of the forehead. So, to begin to understand Neptune, one must use imagery and visualization, step out of the world of fact and reason and into the world of creativity, illusion and magic.

When Neptune enters one's life, a number of things begin to happen. Suddenly, the world doesn't seem real anymore; nothing is concrete. Doubts and confusion may begin to arise regarding one's purpose or direction. Tapping into one's source or center begins to dominate all activity, creating a thin veil between the person and his environment. Neptune asks that you go within to find the answers, and when one is experiencing Neptune, that seems to be the only true reality. One needs space, has urges to manifest something of significance from within his soul and often taps into his creative wellspring of talent at that time.

In relationships, Neptune can be quite selfish. Oh, yes, it's the one everyone looks to for the "soulmate," the perfect union. But in the process of selecting that very special one who will pay attention to your every wish, whim and fantasy, the desire often becomes addiction and the bond becomes bondage. Be careful with Neptune. Its job seems to be to fool you, and it does its job quite well. It may be beautiful when you're drunk, drugged or in deep dreamland (all of Neptune's domain), but when you come out of it, take another look and make sure.

In relationships, Neptune seeks a special (some call it spiritual) awareness and psychic bond between two people, as if an imaginary cord were tying them together. Neptune's energies describe the urge to merge and become one. I have seen numerous marriages take place at the time Neptune crosses the angles of the natal or composite chart. With Neptune, a couple seeks to understand the essence of the relationship: why are they together, and where are they going? They will go to psychics and regressionists seeking to find out how and where they were together in past lives. If is not the question (they are totally convinced they were together). They will see and hear what they want to hear about their partner, regardless of whether that's what is happening or not.

It should come as no surprise, then, that Neptune contacts between couples who live together, marry and choose to see themselves as soul mates are frequent. How could it be any other way?

If you come around a person whose Neptune is the strongest sender into your chart, you may never totally see the truth about them. You will only see what they want you to see. They may lie to you, space you out, take you to another universe or mystify you with their acute ability at art, music or drama, but you will be totally convinced that something about them contains magic.

NEPTUNE/NEPTUNE

Most couples have the conjunction of their Neptunes, since it stays in a sign approximately 14 years. The conjunction of the two Neptunes says they are from the same generation, one whose ideals, longings and creative urges seek a similar outlet. Neptune governs music, and the 14-year transit of Neptune through a sign usually has a generation captivated and connected to each other through the same musical trends if for no other reason, as they are individually and collectively tuning into and receiving the same melodies and rhythms as their peers. A close conjunction of two Neptunes may also enhance awareness of each other on subtle planes - an increased ability to feel what the other is instinctively feeling. They also share the same addictions. A Neptune in Libra person would never ask another Neptune in Libra person WHY he smokes pot; he understands perfectly well. But a Neptune in Virgo person whose favorite escape might be martinis may have problems understanding the desire for marijuana.

When the Neptunes are in a square or semi-square aspect to one another there may be some confusion or misunderstanding between two people in what they see as a realistic goal or attitude, but they will be drawn to each other nonetheless.

NEPTUNE/PLUTO

The conjunction of the two distant-most planets in our solar system occurred in the 1890's in the sign Gemini, a sign that deals with short trips, travel and communication. This conjunction initiated a period of history that will be remembered most for the automobile, the telephone and the impact those industries have had in making the world a lot smaller.

Neptune, the ruler of Pisces, blends with Pluto, the ruler of Scorpio, to bring together that which is beyond the everyday routine to delve into much deeper causes. Both operate on a subconscious plane of feeling and Neptune acts as a receiver for Pluto's ability to strongly send. Pluto would be responsible for engineering deep, lasting changes within Neptune, while Neptune would have a soothing, relaxing, possibly spaced out affect on some of Pluto's intense energy.

For the last half of the 20th Century, these two bodies have been in a sextile aspect to one another, so many couples have the sextile in their own charts and with their mates. The sextile is an aspect that suggests opportunity for harmonious interaction, which is quite fortunate. You wouldn't want to witness the effects of a world trying to peacefully co-exist with these two bodies in a tense aspect. We have enough problems trying to peacefully co-exist as it is and we need all the help we can get. Additionally, this 50-year aspect between the ruler of the underworld and the underwater have produced a world intent on discovering some of the deeper aspects of the psyche and soul.

Additionally, the conjunction of one's Neptune to another's Pluto has been occuring for most of the 20th Century between parents and their children - one generation to the next (parents = Neptune, children = Pluto). Since the movement of Pluto speeds up toward the end of the century, the age gap will narrow from about 30 years to approximately 15 years apart. This relationship may have the Neptunians (adults) finding many of their belief systems being challenged by their children, the Plutonians, as Pluto attempts to both challenge, change and break down old systems that no longer are useful to society. This occurs both individually and collectively and has contributed a great deal to the generation gap children feel towards their parents and vice versa.

NEPTUNE/NODE

There is a strong affinity between these two, as Neptune seeks to define our soul's purpose for being here, while the Nodes reflect the road our souls are traveling - where we've been and where we are headed. This pair seems to be the one everyone looks for in the soul mate mania that is the current rage.

When they meet, they do not need to speak. It is as if they "see" each other on another level - another time or place, another body. There is something quite mysterious about this union - neither of them know what - they just know they cannot avoid being with each other until they understand their purpose for togetherness. The Node is quite susceptible under Neptune's hypnotic influence and will usually go along for the ride. It is almost as if it cannot resist going along for the ride, as if it was being swept away by some magical, invisible force. Yet it is the Node who will record this experience in the annals of soul voyages as one of the most meaningful, for better or worse, of their entire existence.

NEPTUNE/ASCENDANT

The conjunction of one's Neptune to another's Ascendant is quite frequent in all kinds of meaningful relationships. Neptune has a way of tuning into and responding to the Ascendant and in turn, exerting a magical influence over the Ascendant. Often this relationship is based on a "victim/saviour" kind of interplay, in which one is seeking to help or save the other person from some form of self-destruction. It can be a highly idealized relationship. The Ascendant needs to look clearly at what Neptune is asking for and Neptune needs to be aware that Ascendant is, after all, human and imperfect. Yet the frequency of these contacts between loved ones seems to indicate there is a great need to be with each other, and for better or worse, is one that usually endures.

NEPTUNE/MIDHEAVEN

Neptune very often falls on or near the Midheaven for friends and business associates and in opposition to the Midheaven for married couples and lovers (thus falling around the Nadir). This is a contact point that seems to need a definition for what they are doing or where they are going. They will help answer these questions for each other. There is a great deal of sensitivity here, often artistic, musical and mystical experiences that are shared.

When Neptune is near one person's Midheaven, it may manifest the utmost in creative, spiritual and helping professions. When Neptune opposes the Midheaven, there may be an emphasis on the nurturing and protective aspects of the relationship and a deeply felt spiritual bond is being cemented.

PLUTO

"We can change the world
Re-arrange the world
It's dying
To get better..."

Graham Nash
"Chicago"

RULER OF: SCORPIO (8)   PRINCIPLE: immortality, death
and rebirth, transformation,
change from within, power and
control

WHAT IT REPRESENTS:

Pluto, the slowest moving planet with the largest orbit to complete around the Sun, is but a tiny dot in the solar system when compared to giants such as Jupiter and Saturn. Yet this distant speck in the farthest corner of our solar system has rulership over nuclear power and radiation, which could easily destroy large population centers with but a drop or two. Do not under estimate the power of this planet, which the Greeks referred to as Hades and the Romans as Pluto long before it was ever sighted by a telescope.

Its power in the astrological chart is a symbolic representation of the power it holds in our universe, but we can draw a parallel here. If not well contained and directed, it can be annihilating to those who come within its reaches. Although it stays in a sign anywhere from 12 to 30 years in its erratic orbit, its position by house and aspect is quite powerful. Those having Pluto in dynamic aspect are usually able to wield a great deal of power over others. Pluto's cycle around the zodiac is 248 years, but it moves its fastest as it approaches (1983-84) its own sign Scorpio, remaining there through 1996. Those of us alive during the latter half of the 20th Century are experiencing Pluto moving very fast, one reason why time may seem "speeded up" to many. Thus, we will witness the transit of Pluto nearly halfway around our charts during the course of one lifetime. Whatever planets it chooses to conjunct during that lifetime will be powerfully transformed by the transit of Pluto.

Newton's third law, "for every action there is an equal

and opposite reaction," can well be applied to Pluto. Although Pluto moves the slowest, its energy is felt the strongest. When Pluto transits are experienced, deep changes take place within the psyche, affecting us to the core of our beings. Pluto demands that we let go of old patterns and habits and does not tolerate our unwillingness to do so. If we do not do so willingly, it takes them by force.

Pluto's theme in love seems to be to let go. More people lose loved ones during a Pluto transit than any other time. This includes but is not limited to loss through death. There is loss through a lover or mate deciding they need to be free or need to be with another. There is loss through children leaving home to attain their independence and freedom. These are things that happen all the time, but when there is an unwillingness to let the person go, when there is clinging and attachment, then it becomes loss, and that is how it is defined by Pluto. It is really gain in the long run, however, because part of Pluto's message is to allow that process to happen. "If you love them, let them go. If they come back, fine - if not, they never were yours." So speaks Pluto.

In relationships, Pluto acts like its ruling sign Scorpio. It seeks powerful energy exchanges between two people, not a casual relationship. When others' Plutos contact your chart, they have the ability to powerfully transform that area of your life. If two people come together with powerful Plutos, there will almost always be a power struggle. Like a surgeon or therapist, Pluto will seem to draw out areas from deep within you that are infected, diseased, uncomfortable or vulnerable and force you to look at it in all its glory and then transform it, recycle it and let go of it. Pluto people take pride in that.

If there is a single aspect that stands out among couples of duration, it is the Pluto of one individual's chart making strong contacts to the personal planets (Sun and Moon) and angles (Ascendant, Midheaven, Vertex, East Point) of the partner's chart. It seems that if the relationship is to be a meaningful one for you and change your life in some way, Pluto will be involved.

PLUTO/PLUTO

Nearly every couple has its Plutos together in the same sign, but the closer they are by degree, the more powerful and intense the relationship is. The manner in which they express themselves has a great deal to do with Pluto's natal aspects, because the more potent Pluto person is usually the controlling agent, while the less potent one will steam silently until finally erupting. When two Plutos are semi-square or square each other, the two people will need to exercise restraint and discipline in handling such volatile energy.

PLUTO/ASCENDANT

Aspects of all kinds are very frequent between one person's Pluto and the other's Ascendant in long-term couples. This aspect will result in massive changes (Pluto) regarding how you see yourself and relate to your partner (Ascendant/Descendant). Pluto is the instigator in this combination, seeking to control and often mold the Ascendant into what Pluto wants from that person. the Ascendant will feel a strong attraction to Pluto's inner power reserves and will feel strengthened by its relationship with Pluto.

The Ascendant/Descendant axis is one's personal doorway to relationships; Pluto falling there would suggest the need the Ascendant feels to transform itself through this relationship with Pluto. Sex will be a focus in this relationship, as will some intensely emotional highs and lows.

PLUTO/MIDHEAVEN

This aspect occurs frequently in all kinds of relationships, especially those that seem to withstand the test of time. Pluto conjunct the MC indicates powerful partnerships with deeply felt bonds. Pluto will act as the transformer or catalyst for MC's security and status as exemplified in public. In a working combination, this is an effective team. The Midheaven draws on Pluto's inner power reserves and gives Pluto something tangible in return. A close Pluto/Midheaven aspect between two people is undoubtedly an important relationship, one that has the power and ability to change each other's lives.

THE NODES OF THE MOON

"Who knows when we will meet again,
 If ever
 And time keeps flowing like a river
 To the sea, to the sea..."

Eric Woolfson & Alan Parsons
"Time"

THE NORTH NODE: RADU or DRAGON'S HEAD
THE SOUTH NODE: KEHU or DRAGON'S TAIL

WHAT THEY REPRESENT:

The Dragon's Head and Tail have been used by Hindu astrology for centuries, but have only recently become popular among western astrologers. The nodes are not physical, celestial bodies like planets and asteroids, but they are

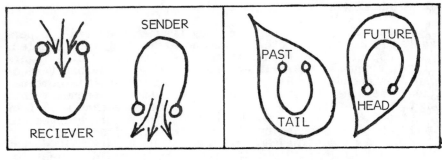

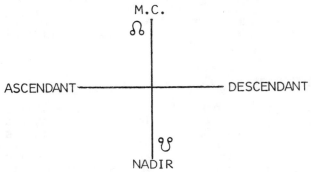

Figure 3-2
The Nodes of the Moon

points on the Zodiac crossed by imaginary extentions from the Moon's North and South poles.

The Nodes' crossroad on the zodiac can be viewed as the road upon which we are traveling. I sometimes view the Nodes as the invisible highway the soul travels upon while the rest of the horoscope constitutes the changing faces and places that appear on that road. Traditionally, the South Node encompasses much of our past and acts as a receiver for all that we have embodied in our (soul's) development. The North Node acts as the pointer towards which we are moving (the future) and allows us to release or send to others that which we have learned. As a team that travels together, then, they work hand in hand. Giving to others by our North Node from the vast amount of knowledge and experiences we have stored in our South Node keeps the nodes well balanced.

The problem, if any, that exists with the Nodes seems to be keeping them well balanced. Many people know how to take and not how to give. Others are givers and do not really know how to receive. Knowing how to give and take, share and cooperate while staying centered in one's personal energies are truly the key to perfected unions.

The South Node seems to keep us bound by the laws of gravity, being the path of least resistance, whereas the

North Node transcends gravity (in a consciousness raising sense). Thus, many prefer the ease and comfort of the tail to the challenge and wisdom contained in the head.

Because the Nodes are associated with the Moon, there is a strong association with the sign Cancer and the Nadir of the chart (see Figure 3-2). The Nadir represents our roots and origins, the point through which we enter the world (through our mother, the womb) and thus ties to the South Node (our past and roots). On the other hand, the Midheaven represents the point toward which we are striving to fulfill a sense of destiny in our lives and correlates to the challenges offered by the North Node.

The Nodes move around the entire Zodiac in 18 years, taking 1-1/2 years through each sign. The nodal axis should not be left out of chart interpretation and should be given as much significance as the Ascendant/Descendant axis when viewing relationship ties with others. In relationships with others, any South Node contact to someone's chart would indicate areas of familiarity – a deja vu of sorts. When one encounters someone with a large cluster of planets around your South Node, you may feel you need no introduction. It is as if you know each other right from the start and there is a magnet drawing and keeping you together. Someone whose planets contact your North Node indicate a growth experience for you. It would benefit you to assimilate some of their attitudes and abilities, although it may produce a challenge.

In most every kind of relationship analyzed, there exists many ties between the Nodes of one chart and the planets or axes of the other.

NODE/NODE

A couple whose nodes are together will share familiar areas in terms of deep psychological experience with one another. They seem to both be working on developing the same potentials while overcoming the same pitfalls. For this reason, they do not seem drawn to each other in the same way that the Node is drawn to other planets or angles.

When the nodes are in opposition to each other, the two people are presented with an opportunity for growth, as the North Node of each person must learn from the South Node of the other. I've seen many relationships that have this reversed nodal pattern, especially in families. Often they seem as if they are going in opposite directions (and they are). But they both have something to teach and something to learn from each other; it is especially nice if they understand that. People with the same node in the same house (i.e., both have North Node in the 6th House of the natal charts, no matter what sign) seem to have a great affinity for each other.

NODE/ASCENDANT

This combination appears often in all kinds of relationships by conjunction and opposition. It seems the souls
have a definite mission to complete with each other. The
two people are drawn together magnetically, having a great
deal to share with each other. They are, in fact, exchanging a kind of energy and experience that transcends physical love - feeling the need to explore the purpose of their
own existence by being a mirror for each other. They will
feel they need no introduction, and often meet in very unusual circumstances that seem highly coincidental. Both
these axes deal heavily with relationships (Nodal Axis and
Ascendant/Descendant axis) and involve an interchange with
people in one's life that seem fated or unavoidable (see
"Angles and Axes of the Horoscope," Chapter 2).

NODE/MIDHEAVEN

This pair in aspect is frequent in couples of all
kinds: married, living or working together. There is an
affinity here with both Node and MC acting as a pointer in
space towards which we are moving. Both people in this
contact strive to encompass the same goals. The methods
they use to achieve their goals are of prime importance in
this relationship. The South Node's conjunction to the MC
offers the MC the chance to benefit from the South Node's
past experiences and know-how, while the South Node is
given a purpose or reason to exercise its nurturing and
care. Further, this relationship seems to enhance parenting that both parties enjoy together - parenting they
offer to their children or each other.

ASCENDANT

RULER OF: FIRST HOUSE   PRINCIPLE: personal identity,
                               outlook, appearance, self
                               interests, the "I AM" point on
                               the wheel; the soul energy

WHAT IT REPRESENTS:

The Ascendant or rising sign marks the beginning of the
First House of the Horoscope. It makes its imprint indel-
ibly felt in each individual, as it defines the exact moment in time the birth took place. This is one reason why
exact birth times must be known for an accurate chart. The
Ascendant reflects the earth's axis rotating completely
every 24 hours and changing degrees of the Zodiac approximately every 4 minutes. It is the invisible but powerful
line that separates past (12th House) from present (1st
House), soul (12th) from body (1st), and defines the person

in a most individualized way.

Almost every astrology text I've ever read has something different to say about the Ascendant, but my feeling
is that its meaning in a horoscope goes way beyond "the
personal mask or how others see you."

It is that perhaps, and much more. It marks the beginning of this life on earth and as such is the individual's
frame of reference for being here - a soul energy. The
Ascendant with its opposition point the Descendant form an
axis in space that separates north from south, daylight
hours from night. This horizontal axis is also one that
distinguishes the subjective, internal experience (below
the horizon) from objective, external experience (above the
horizon).

This axis is of prime importance in looking at charts
for relationship indicators. The natural rulers for these
houses are Aries and Libra, so they will define in a very
personal sense what one is contributing to a relationship
(Ascendant and planets in the First House) and what one is
seeking from a relationship (Descendant and planets in the
Seventh House). Don't overlook planets near the Ascendant/
Descendant that actually occupy houses 6 and 12 but are
close enough to be regarded as Ascendant/Descendant planets. Others' planets falling on our Ascendant will create
an energy that suggests a strong personal identification,
and in fact, almost every married couples' charts examined
contained at least one extremely close conjunction or
opposition to the Ascendant of their mate, that planet
representing the principle reason for their togetherness.

ASCENDANT/ASCENDANT

When two Ascendants contact each other by conjunction,
there is an immediate personal identification with the
other individual. They are seeking similar outlets for
expression and seem to have a lot in common. They usually
experience the same things at the same times (e.g. both
having Saturn transit their 1st House, etc.). Although
they can personally identify with and share the benefits of
these experiences, they do not always contribute much new
information of which the other was not already aware.

There are sometimes extreme personality clashes with
people of the same Ascendants, as they are both trying to
occupy the same space and serve the same purpose. They
will usually strike up a friendship over a similar experience they are going through and may even cross paths over
and over again during their lifetimes, but usually they
will not choose to live or stay together as friends for
long periods of time without the benefit of a third party
interaction. There seems to be a much greater bonding
together of two Ascendants when they are in opposition to
each other than when they are in conjunction. Many married
couples have the Ascendant of one on the Descendant of the
partner.

ASCENDANT/MIDHEAVEN

In five out of six kinds of relationships examined, this conjunction occurred frequently. There is a spark that is felt between these two, with the Ascendant BEING and the Midheaven STRIVING TO BE. The MC often takes on the parental role, while the Ascendant plays the child, as that is what both are more comfortable doing. They will seem to project those roles on to each other. There is a nice interchange of similar personality traits, shared interests and general outlooks on life. They would draw the same kinds of people and experiences into their spheres and often be on the same timing cycles.

MIDHEAVEN

RULER OF: TENTH HOUSE

PRINCIPLE: destiny, goals, image, status, ambition, profession

WHAT IT REPRESENTS:

The MC is an abbreviation for the Latin Medium Coeli, a term that literally means "the middle of the sky." When the Sun is on the MC each day around noon, it is highest overhead, or the middle of the sky. When planets conjunct the Midheaven, they are said to be the most highly elevated in the chart, perhaps exerting the most influence on our ambitions, the point toward which we're striving. It is reasonable to assume, therefore, that contacts to our chart from another's Midheaven would give some kind of association with ambitions, goals and prominence. When one of our planets contacts another's Midheaven, the principle of that planet exerts "influence and prominence" over that individual.

The Midheaven is actually the vertical axis in the horoscope that separates the east from the west. Its placement in the natural wheel is the energy that brings together or focuses the two highest houses in the chart: the 9th dealing with spiritual destiny and the 10th, dealing with material destiny. This extremely important midpoint ultimately describes how both these areas will be realized for the individual.

The Midheaven is the natural ruler of the 10th House (Capricorn's natural house), and as such has an underlying association with the principles of Capricorn. Among other things, Capricorn does represent image, status and ambitions. In one sense, the Midheaven fulfills that role. Another area of concern with Capricorn is parenting. The 4th (Cancer's house) and 10th (Capricorn's house) have always had an association with the parents and family. In some charts, it is the 4th House that represents the mother and in others, it is the 10th that represents the mother, while the opposite house represents the father. In any case, the Midheaven and its association with the 10th House represents a parenting house as well as an ambition house.

Contacts from another's planets to our Midheaven would seem to represent a focus (for better or worse) on our own goals and ambitions. Other people's planets there may either retard and impede our growth, or strengthen and encourage our growth. In any case, we tend to be drawn to them like a magnet because our Midheaven is a powerful receiver of energy.

In relationships between people who are drawn together and stay together, Midheaven contacts are frequent and numerous. People with whom we stay together through time do, after all, have a direct impact upon our future and our destiny, not to mention our status in the world. Therefore, it is a particularly important placement in our charts and exerts much influence over our total being.

MIDHEAVEN/MIDHEAVEN

A conjunction between two people's Midheavens will produce a couple whose goals and orientations toward life are the same. They will see the same issues as being important to them, and they will most likely accept the same values. They will seem to know each other in a way that few other people know them, understanding what motivates them from within. They will also share the same roots (their Nadirs being the same), and probably have the same sets of factors operating in their family conditioning and the way they feel about their families. A strong contact between friends and couples seems to be one person's Midheaven in opposition to the other person's Midheaven. This gives both people a similar understanding, but where one is coming from is where the other is trying to end up, and vice versa.

Chapter 4

SYNASTRY,
THE ART OF CHART COMPARISON

AN OVERVIEW AND DEFINITION OF SYNASTRY

The word synastry is from the Greek root syn, a prefix meaning along with, at the same time or together, as in syncopate, synchronize, synthesis and so forth. In astrology, synastry derives its name from the process of taking two separate charts and comparing them to each other, side by side. Synastry, then, is the art of taking both individuals' charts and comparing them to one another.

In our process of understanding relationships, we know it is first necessary to determine relationship needs, wants and goals in each individual's chart. Typical questions that are asked by people looking for relationship indicators in astrology are, "Is an Aries compatible with a Taurus?" and "Why have I had three Pisces men in my life and they've all broken my heart?" The answers to these questions are sometimes easy and sometimes complex, because there is probably a reason why Pisces fits into someone's chart and becomes a real heartbreaker. Even though we've heard that there is no way an Aries can be compatible with a Taurus (they are both entirely too head-strong and would only clash), somewhere there is an Aries living in complete and total harmony with a Taurus.

Looking at the whole chart of each of the people involved will yield the answer. The Sun is but one of ten planets contained in a chart, not including the Ascendant, Midheaven, Nodal axis and countless asteroids. Although the Sun (sign) may be important in personality expression, it by no means rules the individual. Usually, the sign the Sun is in comprises only about 10 percent of the chart's energy (if not accompanied by other planets in that sign).

When working with synastry, don't forget you are working with whole values rather than parts. For instance, to say Venus in Virgo would be compatible with someone else's Venus in Capricorn only takes into account the sign

113

elements, a fraction of what that Venus represents. To take all of Venus's aspects to other planets, houses and signs gives more accuracy and validity to these comparisons.

Too often we hear signs being compared to signs – is Gemini compatible with Scorpio? Again, the answer to this question depends upon the entire charts. Pure Gemini and pure Scorpio are not what I'd call compatible, but then very seldom are we dealing with pure values. The Gemini may have Scorpio rising and the Scorpio may have Gemini rising, in which case a greater percentage of compatibility may be found.

I prefer comparing planets to planets rather than signs to signs. Let's compare a Sun conjunct Uranus person with a Sun opposition Saturn person. A Sun conjunct Uranus person would be somewhat erratic in behavior patterns, intent of reform and daring to question tradition. The Sun Saturn person would tend toward a methodical, cautious approach to life whose expected behavior patterns would range in the "norm." That aspect alone poses another question. Can they tolerate each other and if so, can they live in harmony with each other by utilizing their inborn differences to complement one another? The tolerance factor plays a big part in compatibility analysis. What one does with the energies contained in their charts, of course, is the key.

Traditionally, the most common method of chart comparison is sign to sign. For example, Charles's Sun (Figure 4-1) is at 22 Scorpio and Diana's Venus is at 24 Taurus, constituting a Sun/Venus opposition between the two charts. House to house comparison also creates a valid picture and may effectively offset seemingly incompatible placements by sign while further enhancing the compatible elements. Charles, with Saturn in the 2nd House, relates well to Diana (Figure 4-2), who also has Saturn in the 2nd House, although they are in two different signs.

Some of the issues I wish to address in working with synastry is the variety of different methods that can be utilized to arrive at the same answers. Remember that we are working with whole values (one complete chart to another complete chart) and not just one piece of the chart.

SIGN TO SIGN: My Sun is in Cancer. Your Sun is in Libra.
My Moon is in Scorpio. Your Moon is in Taurus (etc.)

HOUSE TO HOUSE: My Sun is in the 4th House. Your Sun is in the 10th House.
My Moon is in the 8th House. Your Moon is in the 4th House.
My Sun falls in your 7th House. Your Sun falls in my 7th House.
My Moon falls in your 11th House. Your Moon falls in my 1st House (etc.)

114

ASPECT TO ASPECT: My Sun squares your Sun (etc.).

QUADRANT/HEMISPHERIC: Your quadrant emphasis is 3 and 4.
My quadrant emphasis is 2 and 3.
Your hemispheric emphasis is south
(upper half). My hemispheric
emphasis is north (lower half).

These are some of the many ways to compare two charts for compatibility analysis. Table 4-1 is intended as an aid to be used in comparing two charts and is a good starting point in assessing a relationship.

SAMPLE CHART COMPARISONS

A Comparison between Prince Charles and Princess Diana

The overview of the quadrants shows us that Charles's emphasis is in the 2nd quadrant, while Diana's is in the 3rd. Both are focused in the western (other people, public) hemisphere. Elements and modes yield the chart's signature and we find Charles's fixed (4 planets plus the Ascendant) and fire (3 planets, Ascendant, MC) emphasis produces a Leo signature, while Diana's 4 earth planets and 5 fixed planets results in a Taurus signature. The quality they both share is fixed. While the fixed mode leans toward stability and endurance, too much fixed will result in both personalities being stubborn, unyielding and often uncooperative when trying to resolve something. Compromise is extremely important, as both cannot always have "their way" and cannot always be "right."

There are many similarities between the two charts that work together smoothly. They both have fire Ascendants which indicates they both enjoy the spontaneity, activity and high energy the fire element possesses. Their 2nd House Saturns (both in earth signs) suggest they would view possessions and money in much the same way, and share many of the same values (tradition, heritage and a conservative viewpoint toward money).

Charles has the Moon/North Node conjunction, while Diana has the Moon/South Node conjunction. Both conjunctions deal with the importance of the mother, nurturing and sensitivity in their personal development. Diana's relationship with her own mother and her role as a mother (indeed, the Royal Mom) would be the strong theme in her life. With the Moon/North Node conjunction, Charles has learned from his Royal Mom, Elizabeth II, and continues to learn from Diana many issues surrounding parenthood and family. Tied into this theme is Diana's Cancer Sun and Charles's 4th House (natural Cancer house) Sun. This combination is excellent for working together in a family unit and continuing the family structure as an important issue in their marriage. Charles's key role in fulfilling his

115

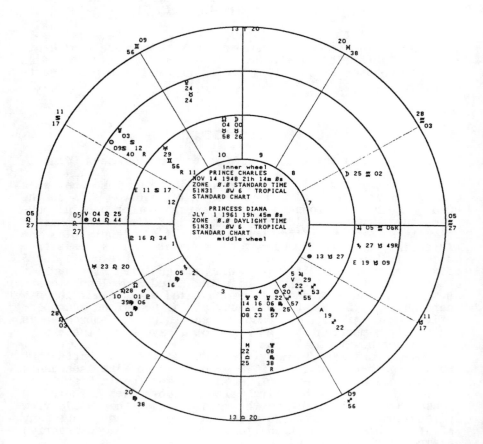

Fig. 4-1

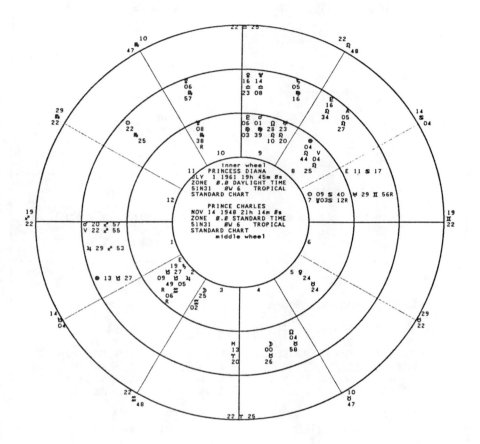

Figure 4-2

Table 4-1
Chart Comparison Form

TYPE: Married Couple	
NAME: Prince Charles	**NAME:** Princess Diana

QUADRANTS OVERVIEW	QUADRANTS OVERVIEW
2 | 0 2 | 6	1 | 5 3 | 1

ELEMENTS	ELEMENTS
FIRE: 3 + ASC + MC EARTH: 2 AIR: 3 WATER: 2	FIRE: 1 + ASC EARTH: 4 AIR: 2 + MC WATER: 3

QUALITIES	QUALITIES
CARDINAL: 2 + MC FIXED: 4 + ASC MUTABLE: 4	CARDINAL: 3 + MC FIXED: 5 MUTABLE: 2 + ASC

SIGNS	SIGNS
Planets, Angles, Nodes:	Planets, Angles, Nodes

ARIES	1	LIBRA	2	ARIES		LIBRA	1
TAURUS	2	SCORPIO	3	TAURUS	1	SCORPIO	1
GEMINI	1	SAGITTARIUS	2	GEMINI		SAGITTARIUS	1
CANCER		CAPRICORN	1	CANCER	2	CAPRICORN	1
LEO	2	AQUARIUS		LEO	3	AQUARIUS	3
VIRGO	1	PISCES		VIRGO	2	PISCES	

SIMILARITIES	SIMILARITIES
1. Fire Ascendant (Leo) 2. 2nd House Saturn (earth) 3. Moon conjunct North Node 4. 4th House Sun/Mercury 5. 6th House Mars 6. Neptune angular (4th)	1. Fire Ascendant (Sag) 2. 2nd House Saturn (earth) 3. Moon conjunct South Node 4. Cancer Sun/Mercury 5. Mars in Virgo 6. Neptune angular (10th)

PROBLEM AREAS	PROBLEM AREAS
1. Fixed Moon (Taurus) 2. Taurus/Scorpio emphasis 3. 2nd quadrant emphasis	1. Fixed Moon (Aquarius) 2. Leo/Aquarius emphasis 3. 3rd quadrant emphasis

own destiny (Moon/North Node in the 10th house, Leo rising and signature) may well lie in producing an heir to the throne. That task completed, he may relax somewhat and enjoy the other arenas that his Leo signature dictates which include royal functions, play, creative pleasures, sports and games.

With Neptune angular (Charles's in his 4th House, Diana's in her 10th), they can be quite idealistic, dreamy, sensitive and truly care about others. Both the 4th House and 10th House also relate to parents, heritage and lines of lineage, which further emphasize the theme of producing an heir to the throne. The importance of a spiritual direction for both of them as well as a deep sensitivity each feels towards others would be highlighted in their relationship. With Neptune angular, there is also joint charisma that made this romance the most highly fantasized and idealized of the era.

Potential problems are shown in this relationship which deal largely with the fixed mode that is highly operative in both charts. They both have fixed Moons which can be highly sensitive emotional trigger points. The stress, however, is somewhat relieved by the 5 degree sextile which exists between the two Moons.

The closest aspect between the two charts is Diana's Jupiter and Anti-Vertex falling on Charles's 7th House cusp (opposite his Ascendant). Jupiter contacts can be nice and in this case provide expansion to him personally, along with kindness, benefit and faith. The Anti-Vertex is similar to an Ascendant, so their opposition to one another can be viewed as energies operating balanced and harmoniously. The Anti-Vertex is usually strongly aspected in charts of couples that seem to "belong together." Diana's Jupiter/Anti-Vertex conjunction also creates a T-square with Charles's Moon/Node to Mercury opposition. They are both used to having what they want, having people dote over them and being the recipient of everyone else's affections. They are learning how to give to each other in this relationship and how to sacrifice their own needs and wants to be the dutiful servants of the public and figureheads of their country.

Jupiter is ruler of Diana's Sagittarian Ascendant and is the focal point of a 5-planet yod. Of course she is learning to make adjustments in this marriage, the main one involving the protocol, behavior and tact she must display at royal functions. This presents a real challenge to her Aquarian Moon opposition to Uranus which typically signifies a crusader for change, somewhat rebellious and quite one's own person. If not for Saturn in Capricorn (doing it by the book) and the strong Cancer, she could be quite controversial to the royal family (and probably will be anyway, once she gets comfortable with her position).

The second tightest aspect between the two charts is Charles's Saturn on Diana's Pluto, which emphasizes the aforementioned need to change the structure. Saturn is the structural agent represented by Charles and his family, while Pluto (Diana) looks for ways to change, manipulate and gain control over that seemingly unmovable rock. The best use of this energy is, of course, taking the combined power they possess and slowly rebuilding the system, step by step, piece by piece, in a methodical, pragmatic way. This works much better than the typical Plutonian method of tearing something down before there's anything to rebuild in its place (see "Saturn/Pluto" section in Chapter 3).

The third closest aspect is the opposition between Charles's Sun at 22 Scorpio and Diana's Venus at 24 Taurus. She brings beauty, art and glamour to his already glamorous (if somewhat stuffy) lifestyle. "As a unit, they would be glamorous and possess a certain aura of magnetism of which others would want to be a part." (see "Sun/Venus," Chapter 3).

Any two charts can be compared, whether they are of people, places or events. Consider a chart for a specific event, such as a marriage, or a specific place, such as a city. Using Moon Moore's Book Of World Horoscopes (1980), it is fascinating to do chart comparisons and composites between nations that often have difficulty with each other. The U.S.A., U.S.S.R. and China can be compared to observe the chemistry that is created between these nations that often spells threat and conflict. The same can be done for other nations that seem to always be in conflict: Israel and Lebanon, Iran and Iraq, Northern Ireland and England, India and Pakistan, etc.

Following is a chart comparison between the United States and the Soviet Union. The same procedures for delineation are used as if this were a comparison between two people. House meanings in a nation's chart are slightly different than in an individual's chart, but the basic interpretations do apply. The main difference is the 4th/10th axis, where instead of being a parental axis, the 4th and its natural ruler the Moon represent the people of the nation, while the 10th and its natural ruler Saturn deal with heads of state, government beaurocracy and so forth.

The 1st House is the actual character and personality of the country, and the 7th House is the relationship it enjoys with other countries and the relationships that are a threat to its existence (open enemies). The 2nd House has to do with the resources and money expenditures of the country while the 8th House reflects the ability to acquire loans and resources from others. The 3rd and 9th Houses are the nation's educational systems, transportation systems, media, press and the roles religion and philosophy play. The 5th and 11th Houses reflect the creative pursuits of the country, its youth, sport, game, hobbies, recreational endeavors and culture, while the 11th House also deals with the Cabinet, Senate, etc. The 6th House contains the armed services of the nation, all labor unions and means of technology, while the 12th House is its welfare agencies, social services, charitable foundations, institutions, hospitals, prisons and the like.

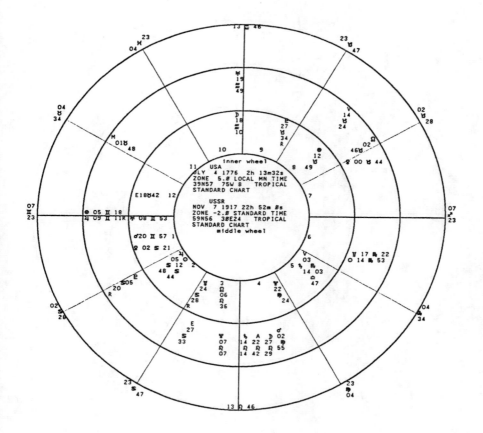

Figure 4-3

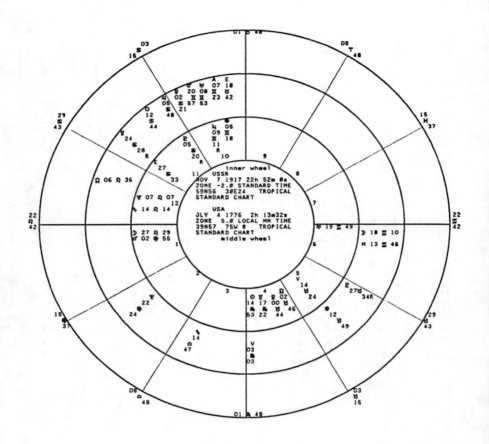

Figure 4-4

A Comparison between
the United States and the Soviet Union

The United States chart is a fascinating look at a country which has grown rapidly. Though many potential charts actually exist for the United States, the one used here (Figure 4-3) for the signing of the Declaration of Independence seems to accurately summarize a psychological view of our nation. With Uranus just about to rise and a Moon culminating on an Aquarius Midheaven, what better statement or declaration for freedom and independence need be made? The natal chart of the U.S. portrays a rebellious, precocious child who through maturity and time gains wisdom, insight and ultimate success. Mars and Uranus in the 1st House of Gemini shows not only the intelligence and precociousness the nation displays towards others, but an impatient "I want to be the first one on the block" attitude of intellectual, technological and materialistic sophistication and superiority. If this attitude seems somewhat pompous, it may also be justified by the four-planet grand trine in air involving Uranus, Mars, Saturn and the Moon. Thus, the technological advancements are spurred on by the heads of state (10th House) and seem to enhance the creative efforts of the people (5th House Saturn).

The vast amount of wealth, natural mineral resources and agricultural abundance is shown by the 2nd House cluster of planets (also called a stellium) in Cancer. Additionally, this 2nd House stellium, especially with Jupiter, implies the capitalist and free-enterprise philosophy that prevails and excessive spending that does take place. Security is one of the most highly valued priorities with so many planets occupying the 2nd House, and with it an innate capacity to accumulate more.

Unfortunately, the Saturn ruled 8th House reminds us that credit extended must be paid for and that there are eventual limits to this excessiveness. Jupiter, Venus and Sun (the pick of the litter) all in one house may seem like putting all one's eggs in one basket. A typical Cancer attitude insures its own plates are always full, and like most Cancers, it will attempt to feed others as well. Never mind that resources are being consumed faster than they can be replaced – the Venus/Jupiter conjunction seems to convey the philosophy that with such highly developed technical skills, a way to correct these problems will be implemented.

A major challenge for the U.S. comes in the form of the Sun/Saturn square, which typically signifies an individual who is of a strict, somewhat conservative parentage, an insecure individual who is too serious about himself, resulting sometimes in an egotistical show of power and strength to hide the deep insecurity. The strict British parent, although overthrown at an early age, still exerted a significant influence and resulted in many deeply ingrained habits and patterns the child has had to deal with. Sun square Saturn individuals normally don't like taking orders from others – they have a need to be in control at all

123

times.   Because it's the square, there can be internal conflict with this principle in its need to express itself as
a super-power. Thus, the ego may be temporarily satisfied,
but relationships with others become quite difficult.

Another challenge for the U.S. comes with its Mercury/
Pluto opposition (3rd to 9th House), the houses that deal
with the press, media, communications and information processing.   Mercury/Pluto has an insatiable need to find out
what's going on beneath the surface, finding it imperative
to snoop around in places they don't belong, deriving as
much information as possible (Pluto/9th - foreign countries
where U.S. intelligence is flourishing). This often results in getting caught and having to pay the consequences.

Mercury is the actual agent that expresses and communicates what is going on, while Pluto poses as the top-
secret, non-divulging, keep-it-undercover planet.   This
might be easier to do if this opposition was any place else
but the media/press-ruled 3rd and 9th Houses. Sooner or
later the plots and secrets will be exposed. The First
Amendment describes the opposition very well: freedom of
speech and press.

It is interesting to note that this Mercury/Pluto opposition was activated by the progressed Sun during the late
1960's and early 1970's - the time of the Vietnam War and
the Watergate crisis. This certainly was an overstatement
of media-ruled events exposing the horrors that were truly
going on undercover both here and abroad, emphasizing the
"sticking your nose in places you don't belong and getting
caught" principle.

The Moon (the people) in Aquarius (freedom/equality) at
the Midheaven (highest attainment) seems to convey the
reason the nation began - as a shelter and refuge for those
fleeing from religious persecution and excessive taxation,
seeking freedom and independence.   It also stresses the
democratic procedures by which we elect our governing officials - Moon in Aquarius - the people's choice. The people
do truly have a voice; whether or not they're heard is
irrelevant.   The fact remains one can still criticize and
attempt to effect changes within the government and not be
condemned, imprisoned or executed for doing so. It is the
democratic process.

The U.S.S.R. is a 4th House Scorpio Sun with a Leo Moon
rising on a Leo Ascendant (Figure 4-4). This triple-fixed
combination implies a solid, persistent, unyielding attitude that is determined to succeed, no matter what. Its
preponderance of the fixed mode and fire element conveys a
Leo undertone to the chart - an energetic, bold sign which
governs sovereignty, pride and sports. With all the Leo
emphasis, it is no wonder the people (ruled by the Moon)
and the heads of state (ruled by the 5th House Venus) channel so much effort into athletics, ballet and dance. The
5th House Venus in Capricorn combines the pure Capricornian
discipline with the beauty and finesse of Venus, with which
they display these finely tuned skills.

Like the U.S., the Soviet Union has a 1st House Mars,
quite competitive in nature with a "me-first" attitude.

Both countries' need for competition with one another show up in many ways. Thirty years ago, the competition was the race into space. Now it is a race to see who can accumulate more nuclear weapons. Even the Olympics have become an arena for this competitiveness between the two countries, whereby their athletes are prevented from participating when one country is angry at the other. When the Mars energy of the chart is not well integrated, it is common to have it manifest as an overdriven competitive need for ego fulfillment and attention.

Other similarities involve the U.S.S.R.'s 4th House Sun/Mercury to the U.S.'s Sun/Mercury in Cancer, along with the strongly angular Moons which both countries possess. This heightened Cancer principle suggests an emphasis on the homeland itself through patriotism, and strong defensive urges to protect its vital resources.

Both countries have a Sun/Saturn square, which literally translated means, "ego conflicts with authority." As long as each country plays authority figure for the other one, the terrible battle between democracy and communism will continue to be seen as "evil spirits" in the minds of each nation's psyche. There is really not a lot of difference between how each country operates, but there is such paranoia by each one about how the other one operates. This paranoia also has some of the Sun/Saturn square fears attached to it. They both want control and are too serious about personal achievements and power. Another paranoia concerns spying. What difference does it make if someone spies on you if you are doing nothing wrong?

Each country also has a strongly angular Uranus, which suggests that freedom, equality and brotherhood, along with revolution, change and innovation are major themes. Both charts were drawn for a time of revolution and both countries seek to invoke an equality philosophy. The difference is that in the U.S. chart, Uranus is involved in a grand trine with the Moon and Saturn, suggesting smooth flowing circuitry between the people (Moon), government officials (Saturn) and the freedom and justice for all principle (Uranus). The U.S.S.R. has Uranus in a tightly bound fixed T-square with the Sun, Mercury and Saturn, implying definite boundaries and restrictions on the freedoms that are allowed. The people of the U.S.S.R. do have lessons dealing with freedom (or lack of it). The involvement of Mercury additionally indicates boundaries on how one thinks and what one says. Their equality philosophy is expressed through socialism or communism. Socialism in its purest form is described by this powerful Uranus, yet the T-square signifies a nation of people who are not really free, although they may be equal. Progress and innovations made are in conflict with authority (Uranus opposition Saturn) and are made slowly, painfully and laboriously, with a great deal of struggle.

The Soviet Union's Venus-ruled MC is in opposition to Pluto (a Taurus/Scorpio energy). This is a somewhat possessive aspect and often collects as many possessions as possible for one's sense of security in the material world.

In this case the possessions are countries, possessing without stopping long enough to find out if the country wants communism or not. The Taurus MC, which deals with money and possessions, is also described by the Venus/Pluto opposition from the 5th to 11th. The constant perceived threat of capitalism and struggle to keep it an enemy of the Soviet Union seems to be the ultimate goal.

The main obstacle to a successful partnership between the United States and Soviet Union comes through the Soviet Union's fixed T-square falling on the U.S.'s Moon/Mid-heaven. The Soviet's Saturn in opposition to the U.S.'s Moon/Midheaven is another very difficult energy with which to work. The U.S.S.R.'s Sun/Mercury square the U.S.'s Moon indicates one whose expression and vitality (U.S.S.R.) are at cross-purposes with the free flowing feelings of the people (U.S.). These same squares to the U.S.'s Midheaven indicate a conflict with the attainment of goals and the ultimate direction of those governing principles and heads of state (communism vs. capitalism). This is further stated by the U.S.'s Jupiter (expansive, extensive) con-junct the U.S.S.R.'s Pluto (closed, carefully guarded). The U.S.S.R.'s Saturn in opposition to the U.S.'s Moon is another trouble spot, as the Moon feels a need to express feelings freely in an open and spontaneous way, while Saturn guards, inhibits and reserves this free flow. The U.S.S.R.'s Uranus conjunct the U.S.'s Moon/Midheaven seems to enhance the attraction these two bodies have for each other, while at the same time creates a need for a great deal of space.

A Comparison between
Elizabeth Taylor and Richard Burton

One of the most highly publicized and media-hyped rela-tionships of our time was the romantic liaison that existed between Elizabeth Taylor and Richard Burton. A comparison of their charts (Figures 4-5 & 4-6) shows many factors which contributed to their "complex relationship."

Because they are both 5th House Suns, they would tend to be "in love with love." Without someone to love or love them, their personal sense of identity would be threatened. Their Suns are trine by sign in the water element, which certainly can contribute to a harmonious relationship, but is not enough if other factors are not present. Examining this water trine more closely, we find Richard's Scorpio Sun tightly conjunct Saturn, while Elizabeth's Pisces Sun is tightly conjunct Mercury and loosely conjunct Mars. Planets conjunct the Sun are basic personality factors that mean a great deal in interaction with one another. The Sun/Saturn personality (Richard) has a tendency to be much more rigid and resistent to change than a Sun/Mercury/Mars personality (Elizabeth). The mutable Pisces (Elizabeth) would be more flexible and probably less disciplined in many areas than the Scorpio Sun/Saturn (Richard). This

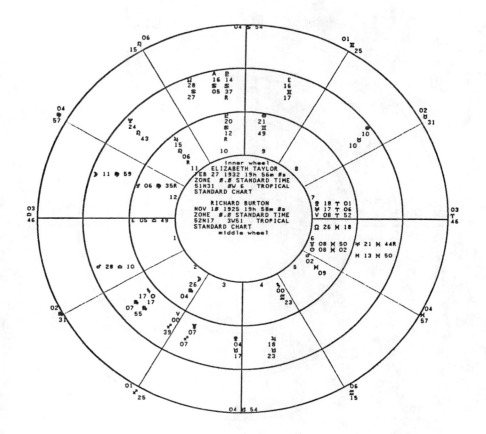

Figure 4-5

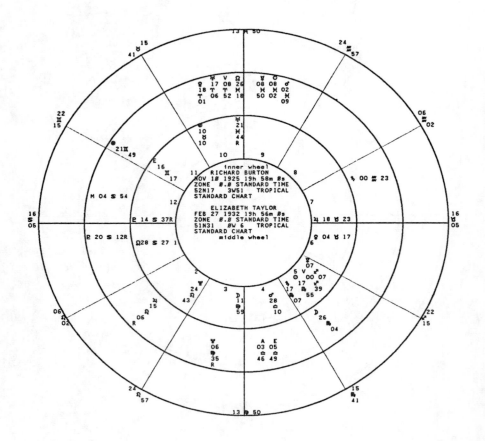

Figure 4-6

128

could be a minor source of irritation to them. A hypo-thetical conversation might have been:

Liz: "Why are you so rigid, so damned narrow and insistent on doing things only one way? You always want to work. Can't you relax and play more?"

Richard: "If you expect to get anywhere, you must work hard for it. There's no time to sit around playing and daydreaming."

The following is a brief summary of their cross conjunc-tions and oppositions. For more detailed information on these planets' interaction, see "Planet-to-Planet Contact between Charts" in Chapter 3.

Richard's Planets to Elizabeth's Planets

Conjunctions:

SATURN CONJUNCT MOON (8:57 orb): It is a little wide, but close enough to be effective. He would tend to say or do things that would hurt her feelings. He would expect perfection from her and want to discipline her. She would want to nurture and mother him, and seek a warm contact. Moon/Saturn contacts will usually show up in relationships of those needing to learn unconditional love. It is an aspect that occurs among many people that belong to the same familiy.

SUN CONJUNCT MOON (8:09 orb): A natural yin and yang at-traction would stimulate and heighten the mother/father principle, the family and domestic activities between them. This is an obvious and powerful attraction. She plays out the Moon, reflecting, nourishing and feeding his ego (Sun) and basks in the warmth of his energy, taking very person-ally his successes and failures.

VENUS CONJUNCT 4th CUSP (0:37 orb) He would add beauty, art and wealth to her home and family that would be an added plus. They would spend a great deal of time and money beautifying their home and enjoying it together.

SOUTH NODE CONJUNCT SATURN (1:21 orb) There's a karmic debt to be repaid along with a lesson to be learned. He paid, she collected and they both learned. She (playing Saturn) would focus on areas where he already felt vulner-able or weak, or felt he couldn't live up to her expecta-tions in that area. This would then cause unpleasant reac-tions in him, possibly wanting to strike back and hurt her in return for the hurt he felt. All in all, this aspect is not too comfortable for most couples, and yet it is as if there is an unavoidable relationship that must take place. It tends to work better when both people have reached a certain level of maturity and self confidence and can understand and tolerate the imperfections that exist in different personalities attempting to live and work together.

URANUS CONJUNCT NORTH NODE (4:34 orb) She is dazzled by his charm, genius and brilliance. They feel the impact like a thunderbolt at first meeting. They need to get used to an unusual lifestyle and erratic changes in their relationship.

ASCENDANT CONJUNCT PLUTO (4:07 orb): He already has an Ascendant/Pluto conjunction. Her Pluto on his Ascendant/Pluto would only add to the intensity they feel for one another. She may try to manipulate and control, but he won't allow it. Potential power struggles may ensue.

Oppositions:

VENUS OPPOSE MC: (0:36 orb): He would add to her status and career image, encouraging and promoting her. He would bring fine art, beauty and elegance to her image. This aspect ties love and work together; they've played many "love duets" on stage and screen.

JUPITER OPPOSE PLUTO (1:49 orb): The sky's the limit – living, working and loving together with a high sense of enthusiasm and adventure that eventually exceeds its limits. They may have felt a strong sense of destiny about their relationship.

NEPTUNE OPPOSE MARS (7:26 orb): Although a highly stimulating initial attraction, the Mars energy often fizzles out when closely aspected to Neptune. There's a difference of energy patterns. Neptune (Richard) may have escaped into drinking, drugs or sleep while Mars (Liz) preferred to be moving, going, doing. He may have felt she demanded too much of his vital energies, physically and/or sexually. The wide orb on this opposition suggests that it was not a major problem area, but that once in a while they may have dealt with these issues.

NORTH NODE OPPOSE SATURN (1:21 orb): Both could relate to working together in a joint business enterprise. They had similar professional goals (and professions) and enjoyed working together. They can learn different techniques from each other as both North Node and Saturn are teachers. The opposition suggests they may resist what the other is trying to teach at times.

MOON OPPOSE SUN (3:57 orb): This is one of the most beautiful aspects for a couple who are involved in a domestic relationship, sharing emotional ties to families. It is a natural polarity, yin and yang. This is a double aspect in reverse as his Sun was conjunct her Moon. This opposition may emphasize their personality differences, with his emotional outbursts (Moon) confronting (opposition) her ego

(Sun).

MOON OPPOSE MERCURY (3:08 orb): This stimulates verbal and mental energy exchanges between them and shows how they liked to play games with each other. It may have resulted in heated emotional arguments, as both the Moon and Mercury are highly nervous and get easily agitated.

A Comparison between Paul Newman and Joanne Woodward

On January 29, 1958, Paul Newman and Joanne Woodward were married. In 1983, shortly after their 25th anniversary, they renewed their marriage vows. Although their signs overlap and the charts show many similar attitudes and habits, they consider themselves quite different. Paul once said their marriage works so well because they have nothing in common. Joanne is a sensitive Pisces Sun conjunct Venus whose passion for dance prompted her to say, "In my next life, I will be a ballerina." Paul is a 1st House Aquarius Sun who describes himself as a "racecar driver who sometimes acts."

Despite those attitudes, they do have many things in common, most particularly their acting careers. They are both multi-talented actors whose films number over 80 between them, but there is a difference. Joanne says Paul is a star, while she is not. Yet it is she who has been the recipient of an Oscar, along with numerous other awards, nominations, and much critical acclaim. They both seek to help and support each other in learning a role, continually striving for perfection in their art.

Elsewhere in this chapter, I mention that a truly great union is one where each person fills in the other's missing signs and houses. In this case, Paul adds very little to Joanne that she doesn't already have and vice versa. Their charts are so similar they must feel like mirrors for each other. Perhaps they are secure in the knowledge that neither one has an unhealthy dependency upon the other; they can both function as well as individuals as they do as a couple.

While their signs and houses may be the same, their planet-to-planet contacts are a beautiful complement for one another, containing the classic textbook aspects one would look for in a marriage or significant relationship. Paul's Aquarian Sun complements Joanne's Aquarian Moon and Joanne's Pisces Sun is on Paul's Moon. (Figures 4-7 & 4-8). There are 25 major cross aspects of 2 degrees or less between their charts. The Saturn contacts are there for stability, time and endurance: her Saturn conjunct his ASC, his Saturn conjunct her MC. The Nodal contacts are there for the soul ties: her South Node conjunct his MC, his South Node conjunct her Aquarius stellium. They have a double Moon/Neptune aspect which produces feelings of the "ideal" relationship: her Moon opposition his Neptune; his Moon opposition her Neptune. Their Ascendants are only a degree apart, creating a similar wheel for both of them.

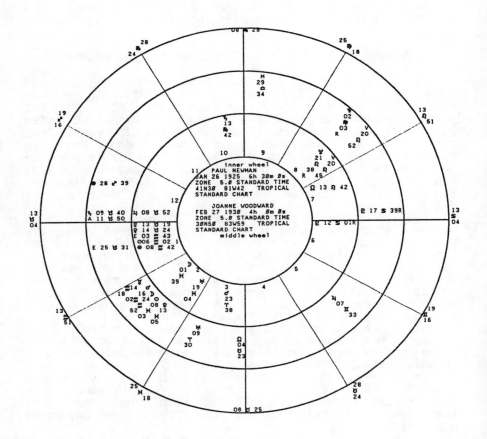

Figure 4-7

132

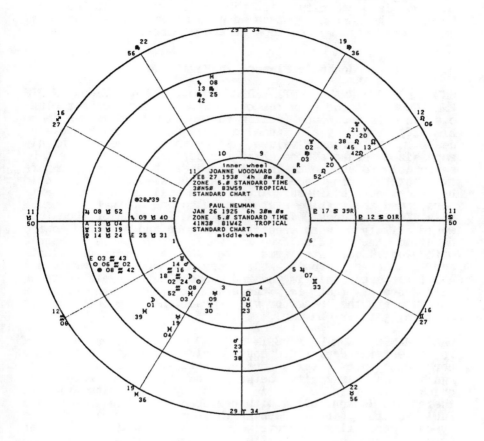

Figure 4-8

(There are a few birth times circulating on Joanne, so this
Capricorn rising wheel is speculative).

Another common way to observe the interaction between
two people astrologically is to place one person's planets
in the other person's houses. While this method can be
used to gain insights into the relationship, it is not
nearly as meaningful as the planet-to-planet contacts
between the charts. But as we have already looked at those
many times, here we can look at the planet-to-house method.

Joanne's Planets in Paul's Houses

HER MERCURY, MARS, ANTI-VERTEX, MOON, SUN AND VENUS IN HIS
2ND HOUSE: Aside from the obvious fact that 5 of her planets in his 2nd House (adding to the 3 he already has there
himself) could yield them a fortune, the 2nd House also
deals with personal values. Since this is the most highly
emphasized house of the chart for both of them, it would be
reasonable to assume their philosophies about money, property, joint holdings and income are very similar. They would
be excellent business partners as well as marriage partners, and their value systems enhance one another. Because
this Taurean house is so emphasized for both of them they
would likely be very security conscious and oriented toward
handling the physical/sensual world very capably. (People
with 2nd House stelliums often have a variety of talents
and resources through which they can support themselves.)
Also, because this is the 2nd House, the emphasis rests on
self-support, that is, there is not a dependency upon one
to support the other or vice versa, they are both capable
of earning their own way.

HER URANUS, NORTH NODE IN HIS 3RD HOUSE: Joanne's Uranus
in Aries in Paul's 3rd House could result in him thinking
her ideas are totally crazy, totally brilliant or both.
Again, the similarity between how their minds work (very
quickly in this case) is shown by both having Aries in
their 3rd Houses, along with her Uranus and his Mars to add
fuel to the fire. Both of their minds work at lightning
speed, generating thoughts very quickly. Additionally, her
Uranus there has the effect of producing broadening and
stimulating concepts, the mind of a progressive thinker who
might stimulate him to open his mind to accept as natural
the world that exists beyond the 5 senses. Her Taurean
North Node in his 3rd would have the effect of counseling
and advising him to think carefully about his holdings, his
monetary investments and so forth. Her North Node in his
3rd would also emphasize the strong link they have mentally; their minds work very well together and encourage constant verbal exchange.

HER JUPITER IN HIS 5TH HOUSE: This can be a highly pleasurable aspect for both of them, as 5th House affairs such
as the stage, self expression, pleasure, entertainment,
children and speculation are expanded and promoted by

Jupiter's presence there. The acting they do together may be more than just a creative outlet or a profession. With Jupiter here it can also be where they expand themselves in every way. Together they are a mighty creative force. Additionally, Jupiter has a philosophical outlook attached to it and these areas involve very strong philosophical beliefs.

HER PLUTO IN HIS 7TH HOUSE: This is a very strong placement for a marriage. Pluto, the ruler of Scorpio, acts out the extremes and goes to the depths and the heights. On the one hand it can be possessive and controlling, and on the other be charismatic, sexual and magnetic. In any case, it occupies a very powerful placement on his angles. Pluto aspecting the partner's angles shows up quite prominently in long-term marriages and in cases of people who have changed the other's life dramatically; this one is no exception.

HER NEPTUNE IN HIS 8TH HOUSE: A highly creative, mystical and romantic interplay would exist between them. This placement reinforces the soul contact they have with one another. They can fulfill each other's dreams and fantasies. Neptune is "screen magic" and in this 8th House of "magic," they would both seem to find an appropriate outlet. Neptune here also adds to a sympathetic understanding of each other's innermost thought processes, a trust, faith and understanding, along with an ability to acutely penetrate each other's psyches.

HER MC AND SOUTH NODE IN HIS 9TH HOUSE: They would encourage each other to pursue their philosophies and get in touch with the meaning of life, supporting one another's belief systems. There is a strong goal orientation with this placement, and they would both reinforce each other's need to accept and complete new challenges in their lives.

HER SATURN AND ASCENDANT IN HIS 12TH HOUSE: Her Saturn and Ascendant fall in one of the most powerful zones in his chart, just above the Ascendant. Saturn/Ascendant aspects are common in relationships that withstand the test of time. It's not just a fling. She is responsible for him and cares for him. She "keeps him honest." He has a strong Saturn principle operating in his chart to begin with (and they both have Capricorn rising), so her Saturn/Ascendant on his Ascendant can complement and further enhance his already inbred sense of timing and discipline. This 12th House placement so close to the Ascendant may also suggest that she can penetrate the layers of his subconscious much easier than even he can do. It is an aspect that often occurs between therapist and client.

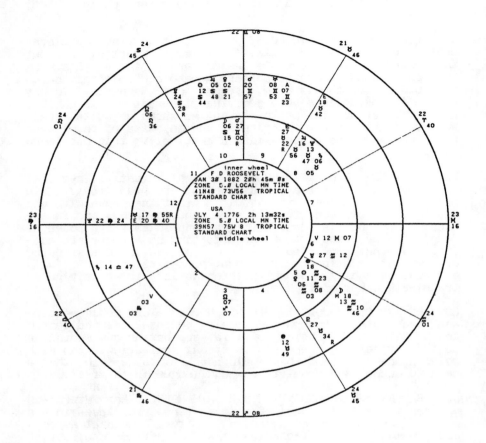

Figure 4-9

136

A Comparison between
Franklin D. Roosevelt and the United States

A poll was recently conducted to determine the all-time favorite, top-ranking presidents of the United States. Franklin D. Roosevelt (F.D.R.) was in the top four (behind Lincoln, Washington, and Jefferson) and the only one of the 20th Century presidents in the top ten.

He is the only president to be elected to the office of the presidency four times by the people. The contacts between the U. S. horoscope and the Roosevelt horoscope are quite supportive of this faith, idealism and honor the people have bestowed upon him.

The Sun, Moon and Ascendant are always strong statements of personal identity in a chart. Here all three points in both charts contact planets and angles in the other's. Figure 4-9, the horoscope of F.D.R. with the United States chart, shows many noteworthy contacts between the two charts. Many marriages examined contain a Neptune/ Ascendant conjunction, and here, the U.S.'s Neptune sits right on F.D.R.'s East Point and Ascendant, close to his Anti-Vertex and Uranus. With Neptune, there is always the possibility of victim/saviour type relationships being played out. When Neptune contacts are very strong, there is the additional likelihood of idolatry, putting one's partner up on a pedestal and refusing to see the person as human and "imperfect." At the time Roosevelt took office, the country was a victim of a depression and needed a saviour to come along and pull them out. Roosevelt's heavy 8th House Taurus stellium was just the answer to the U.S.'s prayers. As he continued to restructure the financial base of the nation, he also became a leader who was worshipped by the masses.

Successful marriages, as stated previously, will have many variations on a theme dealing with contacts to and from the Sun, Moon, angles, axes and nodes. This marriage is no exception. F.D.R.'s Sun falls on the U.S.'s South Node, MC and Moon, while the U.S.'s Sun, Jupiter and Venus fall on F.D.R.'s Moon, all of which are aspects of some significance. The Moon of the U.S. refers to its people, and with it so closely aligned to F.D.R.'s Sun, the people were (and still are) in tune with, and enamored and supportive of Roosevelt's personality expression and leadership.

The U.S.'s Ascendant is located at 7 Gemini, very close to Roosevelt's South Node at 5 Gemini. The Nodal Axis of one crossing the Ascendant/Descendant axis of the partner is another frequent pattern in marriages. His North Node on the U.S.'s Descendant describes the job he had as a mediator and peace maker, dealing with open enemies. There are 25 cross conjunctions from Roosevelt's chart to the U.S. chart. The conjunction is the most significant aspect in synastry, being the cement that holds the couple together. In this case, it held Roosevelt in office until he died and kept his spirit alive in the hearts and minds of the people of the U.S. for many generations thereafter.

Chapter 5

THE COMPOSITE CHART

DEFINITION, CALCUALTIONS AND OVERVIEW
OF THE COMPOSITE CHART

A composite combines the distinctive parts or elements
of two charts into one separate chart. The interaction
between two individuals produces a unique energy field that
has its own "personality" or identity. The composite chart
is a symbolic representation of this unique energy field.
Each composite is totally unlike any other, in that it
would be difficult to duplicate the exact energy patterns
in another person or composite. This is similar to the
chemical mixture of any two elements which when compounded
create a totally new element with its own qualities and
reactions.

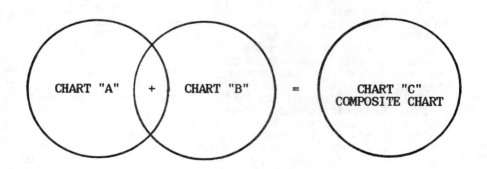

Figure 5-1
The Composite Chart

139

To arrive at this composite, astrology utilizes the 360 degree wheel to locate the midpoints between the placements of the couples' Suns, Moons, Mercuries, and so forth. The midpoint is the composite planet location. For example:

Sun A plus Sun B = C   C divided by 2 = Composite Sun.
Moon A plus Moon B = C   C divided by 2 = Composite Moon.
Asc. A plus Asc. B = C   C divided by 2 = Composite Asc.

A book which is extremely helpful in the study of composite charts is <u>Planets in Composite</u> (1975) by Robert Hand. His study is in the forefront of work on this unique and extremely accurate method of chart composites. In working with hundreds of composites, I have found that some of the techniques in Hand's text work well and others could use revision. I have taken the liberty to revise some of these techniques and offer them here for your consideration. You may or may not choose to work with them, but here are the options.

Guidelines for setting up your own composite chart follow. These guidelines may differ from the conventional methods that have been programmed into most computers. This is important as most, if not all, computers and computer services have a slightly different program for the calculation of composite house cusps and planets. Unless the computer program you are using has the actual midpoint calculations of house cusps written into it, my suggestion is to calculate the composite house cusps by hand from the two charts. You can then make an assessment of the planetary midpoints to see that those are located at the closest midpoint by sign and house. Table 5-1, "Conversion Table for Degrees," is one I have used for years in calculating composite charts by hand.

I recommend that you check the computer print-out of the composite chart against the two natal charts to see that the composite points make sense. For instance, one chart I calculated by the computer showed a 1st House Moon in the composite chart. Both natal charts had 7th House Moons. When you are dealing with two natal wheels whose house cusps are 150 to 180 degrees apart, this sort of thing is a common occurence. That is why I sometimes find it necessary to adjust the final position of the planets to accurately portray the house midpoint as well as the sign midpoint.

Calculating composites by hand has another advantage as well. The relationship between the two natal planets to each other along with the relationship of the composite to the two natals may be more easily seen in this way.

To calculate the composite house cusps by hand is very simple. The Ascendant of Chart A plus the Ascendant of Chart B = C; C divided by 2 = Composite Ascendant. Each house cusp must follow this order until 12 new cusps of houses have been created - or an entirely new wheel.

This is different from almost every computer program I have seen with the exception of the DR-70 Astrological Computer which does calculate the actual midpoints of the

Table 5-1
Composite Table for Degrees

ARIES	TAURUS	GEMINI	CANCER	LEO	VIRGO	LIBRA	SCORPIO	SAGITTARIUS	CAPRICORN	AQUARIUS	PISCES
0 = 0	0 = 30	0 = 60	0 = 90	0 = 120	0 = 150	0 = 180	0 = 210	0 = 240	0 = 270	0 = 300	0 = 330
1 = 1	1 = 31	1 = 61	1 = 91	1 = 121	1 = 151	1 = 181	1 = 211	1 = 241	1 = 271	1 = 301	1 = 331
2 = 2	2 = 32	2 = 62	2 = 92	2 = 122	2 = 152	2 = 182	2 = 212	2 = 242	2 = 272	2 = 302	2 = 332
3 = 3	3 = 33	3 = 63	3 = 93	3 = 123	3 = 153	3 = 183	3 = 213	3 = 243	3 = 273	3 = 303	3 = 333
4 = 4	4 = 34	4 = 64	4 = 94	4 = 124	4 = 154	4 = 184	4 = 214	4 = 244	4 = 274	4 = 304	4 = 334
5 = 5	5 = 35	5 = 65	5 = 95	5 = 125	5 = 155	5 = 185	5 = 215	5 = 245	5 = 275	5 = 305	5 = 335
6 = 6	6 = 36	6 = 66	6 = 96	6 = 126	6 = 156	6 = 186	6 = 216	6 = 246	6 = 276	6 = 306	6 = 336
7 = 7	7 = 37	7 = 67	7 = 97	7 = 127	7 = 157	7 = 187	7 = 217	7 = 247	7 = 277	7 = 307	7 = 337
8 = 8	8 = 38	8 = 68	8 = 98	8 = 128	8 = 158	8 = 188	8 = 218	8 = 248	8 = 278	8 = 308	8 = 338
9 = 9	9 = 39	9 = 69	9 = 99	9 = 129	9 = 159	9 = 189	9 = 219	9 = 249	9 = 279	9 = 309	9 = 339
10 = 10	10 = 40	10 = 70	10 = 100	10 = 130	10 = 160	10 = 190	10 = 220	10 = 250	10 = 280	10 = 310	10 = 340
11 = 11	11 = 41	11 = 71	11 = 101	11 = 131	11 = 161	11 = 191	11 = 221	11 = 251	11 = 281	11 = 311	11 = 341
12 = 12	12 = 42	12 = 72	12 = 102	12 = 132	12 = 162	12 = 192	12 = 222	12 = 252	12 = 282	12 = 312	12 = 342
13 = 13	13 = 43	13 = 73	13 = 103	13 = 133	13 = 163	13 = 193	13 = 223	13 = 253	13 = 283	13 = 313	13 = 343
14 = 14	14 = 44	14 = 74	14 = 104	14 = 134	14 = 164	14 = 194	14 = 224	14 = 254	14 = 284	14 = 314	14 = 344
15 = 15	15 = 45	15 = 75	15 = 105	15 = 135	15 = 165	15 = 195	15 = 225	15 = 255	15 = 285	15 = 315	15 = 345
16 = 16	16 = 46	16 = 76	16 = 106	16 = 136	16 = 166	16 = 196	16 = 226	16 = 256	16 = 286	16 = 316	16 = 346
17 = 17	17 = 47	17 = 77	17 = 107	17 = 137	17 = 167	17 = 197	17 = 227	17 = 257	17 = 287	17 = 317	17 = 347
18 = 18	18 = 48	18 = 78	18 = 108	18 = 138	18 = 168	18 = 198	18 = 228	18 = 258	18 = 288	18 = 318	18 = 348
19 = 19	19 = 49	19 = 79	19 = 109	19 = 139	19 = 169	19 = 199	19 = 229	19 = 259	19 = 289	19 = 319	19 = 349
20 = 20	20 = 50	20 = 80	20 = 110	20 = 140	20 = 170	20 = 200	20 = 230	20 = 260	20 = 290	20 = 320	20 = 350
21 = 21	21 = 51	21 = 81	21 = 111	21 = 141	21 = 171	21 = 201	21 = 231	21 = 261	21 = 291	21 = 321	21 = 351
22 = 22	22 = 52	22 = 82	22 = 112	22 = 142	22 = 172	22 = 202	22 = 232	22 = 262	22 = 292	22 = 322	22 = 352
23 = 23	23 = 53	23 = 83	23 = 113	23 = 143	23 = 173	23 = 203	23 = 233	23 = 263	23 = 293	23 = 323	23 = 353
24 = 24	24 = 54	24 = 84	24 = 114	24 = 144	24 = 174	24 = 204	24 = 234	24 = 264	24 = 294	24 = 324	24 = 354
25 = 25	25 = 55	25 = 85	25 = 115	25 = 145	25 = 175	25 = 205	25 = 235	25 = 265	25 = 295	25 = 325	25 = 355
26 = 26	26 = 56	26 = 86	26 = 116	26 = 146	26 = 176	26 = 206	26 = 236	26 = 266	26 = 296	26 = 326	26 = 356
27 = 27	27 = 57	27 = 87	27 = 117	27 = 147	27 = 177	27 = 207	27 = 237	27 = 267	27 = 297	27 = 327	27 = 357
28 = 28	28 = 58	28 = 88	28 = 118	28 = 148	28 = 178	28 = 208	28 = 238	28 = 268	28 = 298	28 = 328	28 = 358
29 = 29	29 = 59	29 = 89	29 = 119	29 = 149	29 = 179	29 = 209	29 = 239	29 = 269	29 = 299	29 = 329	29 = 359

Remember, when dealing with a circle, there is always a shorter and a longer distance between two points. Always use the shorter distance.

Example: Find the midpoint between 23 degrees Gemini and 14 degrees Pisces:

(1) 23 degrees Gemini = 83
     14 degrees Pisces = + 344
                      427

(2) 427 : 2 = 213.5
     213 = 3 Scorpio

Is 3 degrees Scoprio or 3 degrees Taurus the closer midpoint?
The answer is 3 Taurus.

house cusps. If you use a computer program which can be modified, you might see whether this option can be written into it. Otherwise, the computer will normally ask you to input the latitude of the relationship so that it can find the composite Midheaven and calculate the other house cusps based on the MC degree and latitude. Many people have been using this method without question for many years and seem to find it suitable for their needs. One objection I have to this method is that it does not allow the relationship to relocate without giving them an entirely new composite chart. I think it makes much more sense to use the actual house cusps of the two people involved – calculating the exact midpoints of the Ascendant, 2nd House cusp and so forth all the way around the wheel as a more accurate portrayal of a "true" composite chart.

Table 5-2 shows the composite calculations for Charles's and Diana's charts. Note that the degree of the zodiac is first converted into a whole number based on the 360-degree wheel (using Table 5-1) to help in addition and subtraction. Thus, 5:27 Leo becomes 125:27 and so on.

The Sun, Mercury and Venus are never very far away from each other in geocentric astrology. Because Mercury is never located more than 28 degrees from the Sun and Venus is never more than 46 degrees away from the Sun, they can never make aspects such as an opposition or an inconjunct to each other. It may look a little strange, then, to see a composite chart come off the computer with the Sun opposition Venus, inconjunct Mercury. Here again, you may want to determine the more accurate placement of the three planets as a group by house and sign, keeping them as they would appear natally. Often the house position is stronger than the sign position. In other words, if Venus in A's chart is in the 10th House and Venus in B's chart is in the 8th House, the composite Venus should wind up in the 9th House. This is another advantage that calculating composite charts by hand offers. You may want to run them on the computer to save time, but then check the two natal charts closely against the composite chart to see if planets are occupying the houses that look more closely related. Arabic Parts, specifically the Part of Fortune, should be calculated from the composite chart's Sun, Moon and Ascendant rather than computing a composite Part of Fortune from the two natal charts. The formula for computing the Part of Fortune is to add the longitude and sign of the Ascendant to the longitude and sign of the Moon. From that sum, subtract the longitude and sign of the Sun. Do likewise for any other Arabic parts, novien planets and points that require mathematical calculations to determine.

Table 5-2
Calculations of a Composite Chart

	CHART A: CHARLES	+ CHART B: DIANA	= TOTAL	DIVIDED BY 2	= COMPOSITE
ASC:	5:27 Leo / 125.27	+ 18:46 Sag / 258.46	= 384.12	2 = 192.06	= 12:06 LIB
2nd:	22:12 Leo / 142.12	+ 13:01 Cap / 283.01	= 425.13	2 = 212.56	= 2:56 SCO
3rd:	13:42 Vir / 163.42	+ 21:39 Aqu / 321.39	= 485.21	2 = 242.40	= 2:40 SAG
4th:	13:20 Lib / 193.20	+ 23:03 Ari / 23.03	= 216.23	2 = 108.11	= 18:11 CAP
5th:	22:59 Sco / 232.59	+ 11:01 Tau / 41.01	= 274.00	2 = 137.00	= 17:00 AQU
6th:	3:54 Cap / 273.54	+ 29:12 Tau / 59.12	= 333.06	2 = 166.33	= 16:33 PIS
SUN:	22:25 Sco / 232.25	+ 9:40 Can / 99.40	= 332.05	2 = 166.02	= 16:02 VIR
MOON:	0:26 Tau / 30.26	+ 24:58 Aqu / 324.58	= 354.84	2 = 177.42	= 27:42 PIS*
MERC:	6:58 Sco / 216.58	+ 3:12 Can / 93.12	= 310.10	2 = 155.05	= 5:05 VIR
VEN:	16:24 Lib / 196.24	+ 24:25 Tau / 54.25	= 250.49	2 = 125.24	= 5:24 LEO
MARS:	20:57 Sag / 260.57	+ 1:39 Vir / 151.39	= 411.96	2 = 205.98	= 26:38 LIB
JUP:	29:53 Sag / 269.53	+ 5:02 Aqu / 305.02	= 574.55	2 = 287.27	= 17:27 CAP
SAT:	5:16 Vir / 155.16	+ 27:53 Cap / 297.53	= 452.69	2 = 226.34	= 16:34 SCO
URA:	29:56 Gem / 89.56	+ 23:19 Leo / 143.19	= 232.75	2 = 116.37	= 26:37 CAN
NEP:	14:08 Lib / 194.08	+ 8:34 Sco / 218.34	= 412.42	2 = 206.21	= 26:21 LIB
PLU:	16.34 Leo / 136.34	+ 6:00 Vir / 156.00	= 292.34	2 = 146.17	= 26:17 LEO
NODE:	4:58 Tau / 34.58	+ 29:43 Leo / 149.43	= 184.01	2 = 92.00	= 2:00 CAN

* Answer 177.42 would be 27:42 Virgo. Due to the fact that on the circle there are two midpoints, the closer midpoint which is 27:42 Pisces would be used.

COMPOSITE CHART INTERPRETATION

As stated previously, a composite chart is interpreted no differently than a natal chart. Prominent themes that show up through stelliums, house placements and aspect patterns are, of course, critical to the chart's meaning. However, since a composite chart involves two people instead of one person, the chart is a statement of the couple's interaction. Following are some tips to composite chart interpretation.

"Composite Signs" in the next section refers not just to the Sun sign of the composite couple but to the sign or signs that may be highly emphasized in the composite chart. In other words, any sign that contains the Sun, Moon or Ascendant along with stelliums should be considered important signs in interpreting the composite chart.

Composite Signs

The Composite Aries Couple:

The composite chart that emphasizes Aries describes a couple of dynamic, highly individualistic go-getters and leaders of their own cause. They may not have a lot of friends (unless Aries falls in Houses 3, 7 or 11) but are fiercely loyal to those few they do have. They would have somewhat of an independent relationship, needing to do their own thing whenever they so choose. They may be people who have always gotten their own way and were the focus of attention, so that in this composite Aries relationship they are learning to focus on someone else.

The Composite Taurus Couple:

The Taurus focus tends to be the pursuit and enjoyment of the material world. Therefore, Taurean couples are usually into joint business ventures that had once been a hobby such as cooking, music, or collecting and selling art objects, antiques or rare wines. The fixed and security-oriented nature of this sign is prone to long-lasting relationships and marriages even when they are not working well, since there is more security in staying with the status quo than in looking for a new partner or running the risk of being alone.

The Composite Gemini Couple:

Since Gemini stresses the mental and communicative planes, this partnership will at least have these things in common to have attracted them in the first place. They are both likely to lack follow through in the many projects and ideas they generate. Their home would contain masses of reading material, educational tools and one element of every hobby ever invented. This is a couple who enjoys people of all kinds, and establishing relationships (particularly sibling and close family) can be the principle focus for the composite Gemini couple.

The Composite Cancer Couple:

The couple with emphasis in Cancer displays qualities of deep family involvement, their security-oriented nature centering on the traditional roles in the home, cooking and domestic activities. There is usually a parental role that is satisfied here with both parties alternating between who plays parent and who plays child in the relationship. Additionally, the mothers of both individuals may play a large part in their marriage or relationship. In its most positive expression, the composite Cancer couple is supportive, nurturing, sensitive and loving.

The Composite Leo Couple:

With Leo strong, this couple generally regards their romantic interaction and social life as top priorities, finding many people in their lives at any given time. Because offspring are important, their children (whether physical or mental creations) will figure prominently in their lives. Leo, the sign of self expression and personal creativity demands that they allow time for these pursuits. They may constantly demand attention from each other, Leo being a sign attached to personal ego. Romantically inclined (Leo rules the heart), the small but important extras are necessary: flowers, cards, gifts, surprises and lots of affection.

The Composite Virgo Couple:

They are quite devoted to each other, even if the relationship has failed in one sense or another. The couple with composite emphasis in Virgo may find they do their best work together or seek each other out to help perfect their work, if they can take the constructive criticism each is prone to dish out. They are typically security-conscious, driven by their work or seeking the ultimate from their work to enhance their physical security. Earthy, natural settings are appealing, and they often spend leisure time gardening, farming or in nature's playgrounds. Additionally, their innate understanding of machinery may result in hobbies or pleasures mechanical in nature.

The Composite Libra Couple:

The couple with Libra emphasized in the composite chart involves two people whose combined energy is truly greater

than the sum of the two parts. They share everything including clothing. They tend to be idealized by others as
the "perfect couple." The contented, sociable Libra couple
often pulls others into their romance. Their environment
is usually filled with beauty, music and art.

The Composite Scorpio Couple:

The couple with composite emphasis in Scorpio is often
viewed as extremely magnetic, powerful, often secretive,
and content to let very few others into their personal
sphere. There is usually a strong craving for expressing
themselves through each other, with an intensity and depth
that has not existed for either of them previously in a
relationship. Because their physical realities are sex and
money, these can be dominant themes in the relationship.
Their desire to transcend the physical also results in one
or both of them desiring deep involvement with life's mysteries: life beyond death, psychic phenomena or metaphysi-
cal concerns - planes that sometimes offer a greater reality to the Scorpio than the physical plane.

The Composite Sagittarius Couple:

The couple with Sagittarian emphasis strives to enjoy a
similar philosophical outlook and their lives may center on
creating a perfected lifestyle. Education, travel and philosophy are strong themes, as is the need to earn large sums
of money as an "only the best" philosophy prevails. They
are open and frank with each other (sometimes too frank).
They are often involved with forming new relationships as
part of their growth and learning process and will not settle for confining or restricting, no-growth relationships.

The Composite Capricorn Couple:

Couples with strong placements in Capricorn have a security based, often parental, protective type of relationship
in which family needs seem stronger than personal needs.
They may be viewed as pillars of their community, respected
for who they are and well thought of for what they have
worked hard to produce. Their relationship may go through
many struggles, being somewhat restrained, but will usually
endure through time. Family heritage factors are extremely
strong when there's a heavy influence of Capricorn in the
chart. Others come to them to seek counsel or advice and
it is through others' problems they may see their own relationship weaknesses (and strengths) a little more clearly.

146

The Composite Aquarius Couple:

The couple with emphasis in Aquarius probably has a unique set of principles operating to have formed their relationship and is viewed by many a unique couple. They may be of different cultures, generations or span a broad spectrum of philosophical belief systems. Hobbies and social or political involvements are themes of the relationship, as they are drawn to groups, friends, causes and unusual interests. A unique lifestyle or living situation often characterizes the Aquarius couple. First and foremost, they are friends.

The Composite Pisces Couple:

The couple with strong emphasis in Pisces or the 12th House are in a relationship that transcends the physical plane. They believe their relationship seems destined from the beginning and will often experience deja vu upon first meeting one another, as if they'd known each other in another time and place. Their musical, artistic and mystical yearnings are strong and can usually be seen reflected in their environment. One or both individuals may be playing out a victim-saviour type role with the other, as can be the case with Pisces prominent in the composite chart.

Composite Houses

Ascendant/Descendant Axis of the Composite:

What sign is rising, indicating the start of the relationship, and what sign is setting, indicating how the couple relate both individually to each other and to others as a whole? What are they contributing to the relationship and what are they seeking from it, as individuals and as a pair? Often the sign on the Ascendant, along with its ruler, describes the way in which the couple began their relationship.

An emphasis of planets in the 1st House of the composite indicates a quick start to the relationship, but also a possible quick burn-out. Many planets in the composite 1st house often spells selfishness and competition between the two people, as the 1st house is a "me" house and the composite chart is a "we" chart.

An emphasis of planets in the 7th House of the composite indicates a great deal of sharing with each other, as the 7th House is traditionally the house describing how much of ourselves we wish to share with others.

When these houses are emphasized in the composite chart, there is a very strong relationship taking place. Whatever the length of the relationship is, there is a strong link between these two people.

2nd/8th Houses of the Composite:

An emphasis of planets in these houses of the composite chart puts a certain focus on money, values and resources. Often the couple struggles with the finances, having to deal with who earns what, how the money is spent, is there equality with who is earning what, and which one is supporting the other. Generally, the 2nd House is the earning ability of the couple, while the 8th House may show what earning potential comes in from outside sources (inheritances, dividends and interest, etc.). Too much planetary stress in these houses often indicates an imbalance between how much is earned and how much is spent.

3rd/9th Houses of the Composite:

These houses influence how the couple communicates with one another (3rd House) and what they seek to learn in continuing education (9th). If there is a strain in communications, it usually shows up in the 3rd House planets or the planetary ruler of the 3rd House receiving stressful aspects.

These houses additionally influence both individual's families, as the 3rd House deals with siblings and the 9th House deals with in-laws. Stressful aspects from 3rd to 9th or 4th to 9th House planets may indicate a strain in dealing with the partner's family due to possible communications problems or entirely different philosophical or religious backgrounds.

Nadir/Midheaven Axis of the Composite:

The Nadir symbolizes our roots. form where we are coming. In a sense, it describes family blood ties and one's early beginnings. Thus, planetary emphasis in a composite 4th House indicates strong family ties for both partners, and often suggests that they would be establishing a family of their own. There is generally a lot of involvement with parenting, providing for one's family and caring for the home when composite planets occupy the 4th House.

The MC and 10th House is also a parenting house, but more in the sense of the disciplining or teaching parent role. It has to do with the couple's orb of influence within society (their professional life and/or status within the community). When composite planets occupy the 10th House, there is a greater need by the copule to fulfill the external role outside the home. When stressful aspects occur between the 4th and 10th House planets in the composite, there may be a strain between how much time is spent at home with family and how much the couple puts into their professional life.

148

5th/11th Axis of the Composite:

These houses put strong emphasis on relationships with other people, as they are fun-loving and people-oriented. The 5th House is more specifically the house of relationships with children and close contacts of the heart, while the 11th represents relationships with friends and the peer group with which the couple identifies. Emphasis in the 5th House suggests the couple's attitudes about children, their relationship with them and how they are raised, or if they even want children. The creative 5th House, if not procreation, deals with the couple's own creative pursuits: sports, hobbies, entertainment, recreation, pleasure, speculation and so forth. This house will show how they achieve those outlets.

Emphasis in the 11th House deals with the friends and groups of people with whom they associate. What peer group do they identify with: the condo crowds at the ski resort, ballet and theater crowds or race car drivers? The 11th House is usually one of friends, while the 5th House is one of lovers. When an emphasis of planets fall in the 11th of the composite, the couple should be prepared to "let the partner go" and not try and put boundaries or expectations upon each other. Stressful aspects between these two houses will often play out a scenario dealing with possessive love (5th) and detached love (11th).

6th/12th Axis of the Composite:

These houses generally represent areas of service to each other. Planets occupying the 6th House indicate an emphasis in the couple's working relationship with each other. Can they work together, do they enjoy sharing work with each other and do they have the same set of principles operating in their daily routine? It is also a house of perfection (being Virgo's natural house) and stressful aspects to planets in this house may indicate expectations of perfection that one partner places upon the other.

The 12th House has to do with the privacy the couple seeks with each other within their relationship. Unconscious factors that motivate and catalyze the relationship are contained within the 12th House, as well as a feeling of "we've been together before" or "we belong together." On the other hand, if there are serious blocks preventing one individual from truly understanding the other, that will also show up in the 12th House of the composite, as the 12th House can deal with factors in the subconscious that have not found a way to surface.

Composite Planets

Sun Position:

The life force and vitality of the relationship is usually indicated by the Sun. Because the Sun is also associated with the masculine, archetypal yang energy in a chart, its position in the composite chart very often describes the more masculine element of the relationship. In composite charts where there are a man and a woman playing out traditional roles, the Sun usually describes the man. If, however, the couple are of the same sex or there is a role reversal, the Sun describes the more forceful of the two people as well as the ego identity of the couple. Many stressful aspects to the composite Sun or a Sun that is weakened by sign or house position usually indicates some difficulty in self expression (either too much or not enough) by the male element.

Moon Position:

The sensitivity, nurturing and caring of the relationship is often indicated by the Moon. Whereas the Sun is the active, forceful one, the Moon plays out the reactive role and usually describes the mothering, feminine force of the relationship. In the majority of couples' charts that I've examined, this is usually, but not always, a woman. In composite charts of the same sex, there is often one person who will play out this Moon role more naturally than the other. When the Moon of a composite chart is stressed, there is often a problem with the emotional expression in this relationship. With Moon square Neptune, she may easily delude herself into seeing what she wants to see and not what is really going on. A Moon square Saturn might indicate a controlled, stiff emotional environment where expressing one's feelings is very difficult. In short, the Moon position indicates not only the sensitivity and nurturing of the relationship and how these two individuals express their needs for fulfillment, but more specifically the woman's role in this union. Once again, if the couple is the same sex or there has been a sexual role reversal, the Moon will describe the person who has become the "mothering" force in the relationship.

Mercury:

The communication element is denoted by Mercury. Are the two speaking the same language? What language are they speaking? This is an important indicator in compatibility analysis and in the composite chart, as it is often the first connection the two people make with each other. How does Mercury aspect the rest of the chart?

Venus and Mars:

This planetary pair, like Sun and Moon, represent a male and female yang and yin force interacting. With Venus and Mars, however, the expression is on the social/sexual plane, adding romance to the relationship. Note how Mars and Venus aspect each other, if at all, what sign/house placement they hold and how each aspects other planets and points within the chart.

Jupiter and Saturn:

This planetary pair is concerned with broader-based interests. How does the couple relate to society at large? What are they contributing (Jupiter) to the relationship and what is their relationship contributing to others? What are they learning to deal with in each other (Saturn)? As a couple, are they able to bear all the responsibilities they have without too much stress (Saturn) and can they enjoy that for which they have worked (Jupiter)? Can they share their belief systems and philosophies of life with one another (Jupiter)?

Uranus, Neptune, and Pluto:

This transcendental trio looks beyond the everyday concerns into greater understanding and expansion. Uranus, Neptune and Pluto closely aspecting the angles of the composite indicate that this couple has made a significant impact upon one another and that the relationship is bigger than both of them. They are learning and sharing something with each other that has to do with soul growth.

Again, we first look to each individual's chart to see what role these planets play natally. A closed circuit connection of these planets (aspects linking each other to many other planets and angles in the horoscopes) implies a significant relationship, and often one that changes both their lives.

Clusters and Stelliums:

Composite charts have a way of creating clusters of planets in one area of the chart. This is known as a stellium. What house and sign is the stellium located in and what is the couple experiencing with this placement? The major issues the couple is dealing with will usually be emphasized by the sign and house position of the stellium.

Power Points:

Are there composite planets located in these zones? These zones of the chart are the areas ten degrees either side of the four angles: the Ascendant, Descendant, Midheaven and Nadir (see "Angles and Axes of the Horoscope," Chapter 2 for more information about power points.) The planets located in these zones often express themselves strongly, and are focal indicators of major themes in the composite chart.

The main thing to remember when interpreting a composite chart is that it is really no different than interpreting a natal chart, except that we are dealing with a pair rather than an individual. In an individual's natal chart, when there are challenging aspects and situations shown that must be worked out, the individual has no choice but to work them out, even if it takes one's whole life to do so. What else is he/she here for and where is one going to go to escape those challenges? However, if the composite chart shows those same challenging situations to work out, it is much easier to leave than to try and work them out. This makes the composite chart a little bit trickier to work with, in that if the patterns created by the two people are not for the most part stable and harmonious, the couple either chooses to avoid one another or remains together for a relatively short time.
Another key to composite chart interpretation is in noting the important placements and aspects of planetary energies that are uniquely different from the two natal charts. What does this chart state that is absent in the natal chart? If the two people were born with a Saturn/Neptune conjunction, the composite will also contain the Saturn/Neptune conjunction. This is not significant. What is significant is the house placement of this conjunction and the aspects it makes in the composite chart to other planets or angles that are not found in the natal charts.
The same is true when comparing any important aspect in the composite to any important aspect in the natal. One composite chart I studied is that of a couple who had met and instantly fallen in love. The composite chart contains a T-square in the fixed mode linking Mars, Venus and Pluto (Was it love or lust?). In the man's chart, there is nothing even close to this aspect pattern or degree. However, this composite T-square falls directly on the woman's natal square of Venus and Mars. She is under much stress in this relationship, worrying that it will dissipate at any moment. She is hanging on for dear life and every time he says good night, she is in mortal fear that he means good-bye. Learning to let go and overcome the fears raised in the relationship by the Mars/Venus/Pluto T-square is quite important for her. Because he does not have the aspect, he does not have to deal with the problem. Therefore, it is also difficult for him to understand why she overreacts. This is one example of the importance of comparing the composite to each of the individual's natal charts.
A composite chart not only contains the elements of personal interaction between each individual, but also their

relationship with the world at large. I have chosen for my examples of composites two pairs who not only influenced each other a great deal, but left a significant mark on the world around them – John Lennon and Paul McCartney, and Paul Simon and Art Garfunkel.

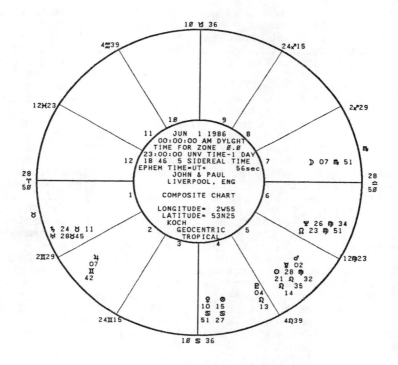

Fig 5-2

The Composite Chart of
John Lennon and Paul McCartney

The music that hit the airwaves with "Yeah, yeah, yeah" evolved into some of the most potent social, political and spiritual proclamations of the century, turning on a whole generation of people. The two individuals responsible for composing and performing this music were John Lennon and Paul McCartney. There are some powerful themes contained in their composite chart (Figure 5-2).

The Leo theme is quite apparent with four planets in Leo's sign and four planets in Leo's house, including its own ruler, the Sun; superstars, they were. A Sun/Mercury conjunction in a composite can most certainly indicate a marriage of the minds. The earth trines from Houses 1 to 6 indicate a potentially excellent working relationship. The fixed squares from 1 to 5 indicate a potentially troublesome ego and personality struggle. The square from Mercury to Uranus is exact; the square from Sun to Saturn is close. The chemistry Lennon and McCartney created through their music erupted into a cultural revolution (Uranus), powerful enough to threaten the traditional concepts and values (Saturn) that existed at the time. They became synonomous with the turbulence and youth rebellion that captured and earmarked the 1960's. But they were not just revolutionaries. This chart contains several earth trines between the North Node/Neptune conjunction in Virgo and the Saturn/Uranus conjunction in Taurus. Among other things, earth trines can be a strong ability to master the material world. They did have a profound effect on the masses, and what is particularly striking about their composite chart is how the Neptune/North Node conjunction pointed to the part they were destined to play in "awakening" the masses. If the North Node is truly a vehicle through which we play out what we are here to learn, its conjunction to Neptune and its placement in the 6th House suggests their role as spiritual gurus was part of their work. Their music became spiritual chants that unified a generation of people seeking to go along on "The Magical Mystery Tour." Their music raised people's consciousness, and although they unintentionally created a schism between the generations, with time even the older generation found themselves humming Beatles' tunes to the elevator Muzak systems.

The 7th House Scorpio Moon trines Venus in Cancer. This describes the emotional sensitivity, attunement and psychic connection they had with one another, along with the powerful mesmerizing effect they had upon their public. The public could not tolerate their split-up, and many plots and plans by the media to reunite them failed. With such super-star status and all of this talent, how is it their partnership dissolved?

For one thing, the tight fixed squares between the 5th House Sun/Mercury and 1st House Saturn/Uranus must have been a terribly heavy ego burden to carry around. It demanded them to always smile for, and perform and cater to an unrelenting public. Sun/Saturn squares in composites often play out authority figure roles for each other. There is usually an underlying insecurity with Sun/Saturn. Sun/Uranus squares offer strong magnetic attractions, but also present inconsistent behavior patterns and create constant desire for change. The Saturn/Uranus configuration itself can be very demanding: two super heroes or gods who need to respect each other's "divinity." (see Chapter 3, SATURN/URANUS).

Another problem area of the chart is depicted by the Scorpio Moon squaring its ruler, Pluto. While this aspect

has the ability to mesmerize the masses, it does not bode
well for a personal relationship. This Scorpio planet
square its own sign indicates an underlying power struggle.
One would need to change the other; one would always need
to maintain control. Moon/ Pluto aspects work like a
vacuum. There is an incredible suction force drawing the
two people together and holding them there. It involves
two people in a relationship who descend to the emotional
depths and ascend to the emotional heights together. While
its chemistry produced powerful music that had the ability
to change mass consciousness, its negative manifestations
in the personality level dealt with possessiveness and
manipulation which eventually led to their dissolution.

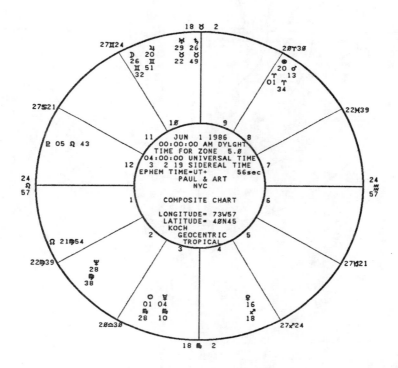

Figure 5-3

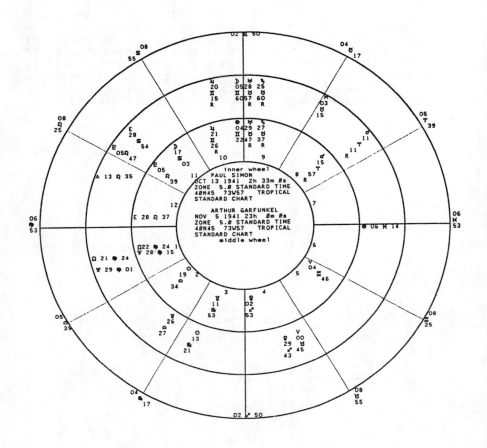

Figure 5-4
Horoscope of Paul Simon

156

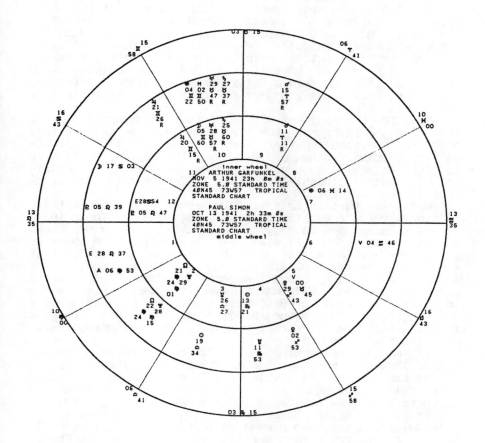

Figure 5-5
Horoscope of Art Garfunkel

The Composite Chart of
Paul Simon and Art Garfunkel

Like the Beatles, Simon and Garfunkel became living
legends during the 1960s, a time when a whole generation of
people looked to pop music and its songwriters for their
spiritual guidance. Several themes that were apparent in
the Lennon/McCartney composite are also contained in the
Simon/Garfunkel composite (Figure 5-3). Both contain a
Sun/Mercury conjunction - in Lennon and McCartney's it was
in the 5th House; here it is in 3rd House Scorpio. Both
composites also contain a Saturn/Uranus conjunction trining
a Neptune/North Node conjunction and a square to Pluto from
its Scorpio planets.

The Sun conjunct Mercury in Scorpio would again suggest
the close merging of the minds into one, so that as they
sing and perform together, they have the ability to create
an incredible fusion and harmony. The Neptune/North Node
conjunction is also present, portraying them also as musical missionaries, with the ability to feed millions of spiritually starved youth.

What is particularly striking about this pair is their
30-year love/hate relationship with each other. Their individual charts are equally as striking since they were born
so close together (Figures 5-4 and 5-5). Born the same
year, one month apart, even the signs of their Ascendant
are only one sign apart. With the exception, then, of the
inner planets Sun, Moon, Mercury and Venus, their charts
are very similar. Even with these differences, Simon's Sun
in Libra is conjunct Garfunkel's Mercury, and Garfunkel's
Sun in Scorpio is conjunct Simon's Mercury. Like identical
twins, they are mirrors for one another, not always happy
with the reflection.

In an interview Simon said, "There's a sense of competition between us that dates from the beginnings of our
friendship, at age 12. This is a friendship that is now 30
years old. And the feeling of love parallels the feeling
of abuse..." (Playboy magazine, February, 1984, p. 163.)

Paul and Artie began as a couple of adolescent school
friends in Queens, who played music together but eventually
became a business partnership and legend known as "Simon
and Garfunkel." The unfortunate thing for them, similar to
the Lennon/McCartney composite, was that the personal harmony of their relationship was non-existent except in their
music and the minds of millions of loyal fans. There were
terrible power struggles between them that could not withstand the pressure of being together. They loved their
music, but intensely disliked each other.

Paul Simon's Chart (Figure 5-4) contains a very close T-
square between Sun, Moon and Mars, an aspect that makes
close personal relationships challenging, if not downright
impossible. This T-square describes one who struggles to
create a powerful personal identity (Sun opposition Mars)
only to react to it later (both planets square the Cancer
Moon). Add to this a Venus opposition to Saturn and Uranus
and you get a person who is extremely hard to live with -

the gifted but temperamental artist syndrome. Meanwhile, Art Garfunkel's chart contains a T-square involving Venus at 29 Sagittarius, Neptune at 29 Virgo and the Anti-vertex at 0 Cancer, a configuration that describes the dreamer looking for the impossible "ideal" relationship. They could not become what the other wanted them to become, although they kept trying to in their turbulent 30-year relationship with each other.

Like the Lennon and McCartney composite, this chart also contains the fixed square of Pluto to Scorpio planets, Sun and Mercury. Although the attraction is overwhelmingly strong with these Scorpio and Pluto squares, the "can't live with him, can't live without him" syndrome is also present along with the Scorpio obsession to make it work, one way or another.

What Paul disliked most about "Simon and Garfunkel" is that they together were always much more loved and adored by their fans than was Paul Simon, even though it was Paul alone who wrote all the songs. The swallowing of children and eventual castration myth portrayed by Saturn and Uranus emerges again.

15 Sample Composite Charts
Briefly Interpreted

The best way to understand composite charts and what they say about a relationship is to calculate and interpret them. A composite chart is interpreted the same way as a natal chart. Keep in mind, though, that this is the chart of two people rather than one. This is an important issue. If a natal chart contains a great deal of stress or tension, a person is usually committed to resolving it one way or another. But in a composite chart, it is much easier to walk away from the other person who seems to be causing the stress rather than dealing with it or resolving it.

Planetary aspects are probably the most important element in composite chart interpretation. Planetary aspects constitute the dialogue between the two people. What language are they speaking - are they speaking at all? What form does their dialogue take and do they understand one another? Chapter 3, the section of this book dealing with planetary aspects, can be utilized for understanding aspects that occur in composite charts. You are bound to find many correlations between the aspects that occur in chart to chart comparison (synastry) and aspects that show up in the composite chart.

What follows is several composite charts calculated for couples who filled out questionnaires regarding the nature of their relationship. Questions were about the length of the relationship, how they met, what they consider the most compatible elements of the relationship and what areas they consider to be the most difficult.

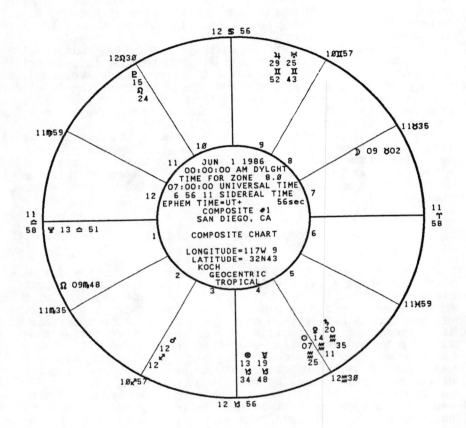

Composite Chart 1

This couple has been married almost nine years. They were married within four months of their first meeting. All the elements indicating love and cohabitation are contained in the composite. A composite 4th House Sun often leads to a cohabitational situation, while the 7th House Moon suggests a deep sensitivity toward developing this partnership as a marriage. The South Node in exact conjunction to the Moon is one of the factors that would contribute to the feeling they have known and lived with each other before. Libra, the sign of relationships, is rising, with ruler Venus placed in the 5th House of romance. Neptune conjunct the Ascendant is a pattern that shows up quite often between marriage partners, either by synastry or in the composite. It suggests a deeply felt bond between the two, a similiar spiritual direction or belief system and a fusing of their energy.

One difficult area for them concerns the handling of the wife's children, which is stated in the chart by a 5th House Venus/Saturn opposing an 11th House Pluto. Another area that poses problems is, in their words, "wife doesn't listen sometimes and husband doesn't express feelings sometimes." An angular Mercury square Neptune is a fairly good description of this syndrome.

A square between the Sun and the Moon, although an excellent indicator for a marriage, can also indicate two extremely different personalities seeking integration. The wife is outgoing and extroverted, preferring the company of others (7th House Moon), while the husband is soft spoken and shy, preferring not to be around too many people (4th House Sun). This 1st Quarter Sun/Moon square may also reflect the difficulty these two have had in establishing successful relationships in the past. The challenge posed by this square deals with compromise and cooperation, including sensitivity to each other's feelings.

The Jupiter/Uranus conjunction in Gemini in the 9th House reflects their love of philosophy, travel and adventure. They travel often and their goals are to retire early and sail around the world.

161

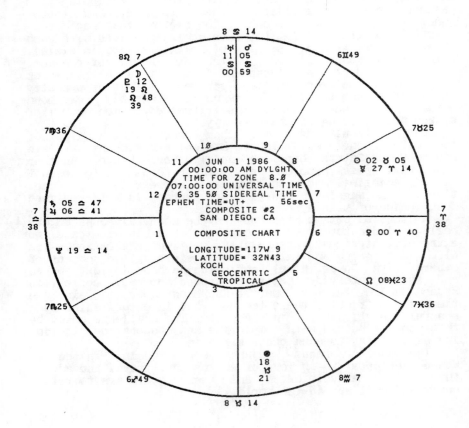

Composite Chart 2

162

This couple has been together for five years. They were married within a year of meeting each other. An emphasized Libra factor exists in this composite, with three planets rising in Libra, the Sun and Mercury in the 7th and Venus close by. Once again, Neptune is conjunct the Ascendant, an aspect that occurs between many married couples.

The timing on this chart was incredible. A Jupiter/Saturn conjunction occurred in 1981 at the same degrees the composite Jupiter, Saturn and Ascendant occupy. This coincided with their time of meeting and setting up housekeeping. The North Node was transiting the composite Moon at the same time. The Nodes frequently come into conjunction with the Sun, Moon or angles of a composite when a major turning point such as a marriage or commitment to one another takes place.

The woman is a deeply feeling person with an intense need for close companionship in a relationship. She is outgoing, extraverted and people-loving (Moon conjunct Pluto in Leo, 11th House). The man in this relationship is an intellectual, seeking to relate on a one-to-one basis with his partner (Sun conjunct Mercury, 7th House).

Venus square Mars is great for a romantic and sexual attraction. This square also pulls in Jupiter and Saturn to form a T-square, and the thrust of this relationship seems to be their careers and their drive towards achievement. Mars and Uranus conjunct the MC in the family and nurturing sign of Cancer emphasizes the personal satisfaction they derive from being in the public and relating strongly as a family unit.

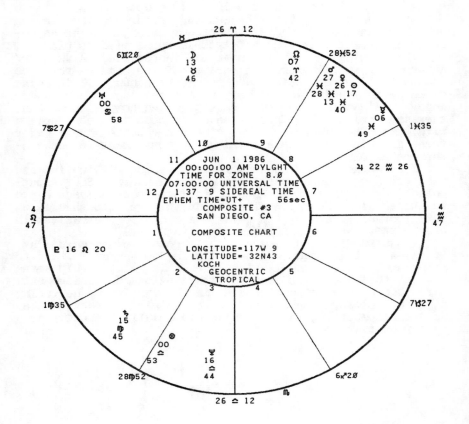

Composite Chart 3

This couple has been together only a short time, but the attraction and marriage were instant. A large cluster of planets in the watery 8th House Pisces describes the mutual sensitivity, sexual compatibility, acceptance, trust and comfort each feels for the other. The Sun is the focal point of a yod between Pluto and Neptune, while in direct opposition to Saturn. For him, the relationship provides many challenges as well as a chance to work out his conflict between feelings and intuition (Sun in Pisces, 8th House) and logic, reason and caution (Saturn in Virgo, 2nd House).

For her, the relationship is a chance to experience the emotional depths she needs to feel and change her pattern of emotional reactions. "The female attempting to run the show" is how they describe one of the more difficult aspects of the relationship (Moon square Pluto in the foreground of the chart). The amount of influence each has on the other's moods ("when one 'hits the pits,' the other has a tendency to follow") is defined by the stellium in Pisces in the 8th House. Yet there is no denying the great amount of inner sensitivity, caring and satisfaction they would derive from being with each other as described by that same 8th House stellium.

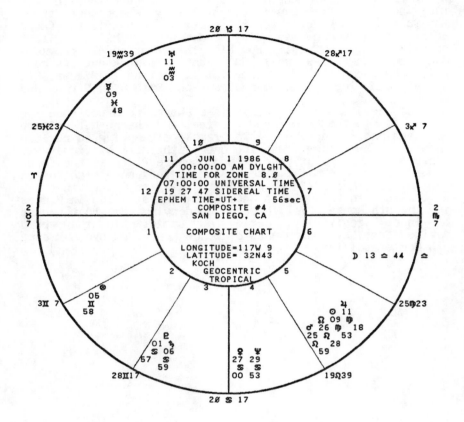

Composite Chart 4

Most of this couple's relationship has involved establishing a home and family (2nd quadrant emphasis) with the
additional emphasis of working together as a team of
therapists (a bucket pattern with Uranus as a handle in
Aquarius in the 10th House). They work from their home (4
planets in Cancer).

Transits to this composite at the time of marriage activated almost everything in the chart. Jupiter and Uranus
were conjunct the Venus/Neptune, Neptune crossed the Descendant and Pluto conjuncts the Mars/North Node while the
South Node transited Saturn. This marriage took place 28
years ago.

The Sun/Mercury/Jupiter conjunction in Virgo describes
the work they do - psychology, as well as describing the
husband - analytical, critical and hard working. The Moon
in Libra trines Uranus in the 10th and the wife describes
herself as the "bouyant, fun-loving" aspect of the relationship versus her husband's more serious side.

The difference in their personalities is described by
the Sun and Moon, but there are similarities between them
which can be seen through the Ascendant and Descendant.
The Descendant ruler, Pluto, is in the sensitive, serious
sign of Cancer conjunct Saturn. The Ascendant ruler,
Venus, is also in Cancer and is conjunct Neptune. This
Venus/Neptune conjunction is one that can be very romantic
or very idealistic.

She describes their past 28 years together as a mutual
respect for each other and an interest in growing together
spiritually, emotionally and physically.

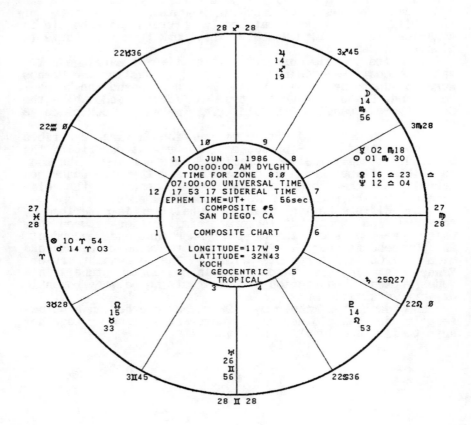

Composite Chart 5

Here is an example of what love can do. Both individuals were in other relationships when they met; she married and he living with another. They met at work and felt more than just attracted to each other. The same kind of recreational activity, mutual support for any new ventures, encouragement for unlimited growth of individual expression and striving to obtain the same goals in the future are only part of what they expressed as the compatible elements of the relationship.

The Ascendant ruler Neptune in the marriage 7th conjunct love-planet Venus tightly opposes Mars. They abruptly had to end the other relationships and find a way to be with each other. They succeeded and are now married. This Venus/Neptune closely aspects the South Node/Moon conjunction in the 8th, Pluto in the 5th, Jupiter in the 9th and Mars in the 1st; love will find a way.

The stellium in secretive Scorpio/8th House along with Pisces rising kept the relationship a "secret affair" until they were able to be together openly. The Sun and Moon occupying the same sign and house are additional indicators that there exists much similarity and a lot of harmony between the two people. The Moon, however, aspects many other planets and its T-square to Pluto and the Moon's Nodes made her experience the emotional tension, frustration and anxiety of ending the other relationships a great deal more than he did.

An exact grand fire trine between Mars, Pluto and Jupiter are indicative of the joint enthusiasm they share for travel, life, adventure, friends and spontaneity. The marriage took place when Neptune, the Ascendant ruler conjuncted the Midheaven and squared the Ascendant/Descendant of this composite.

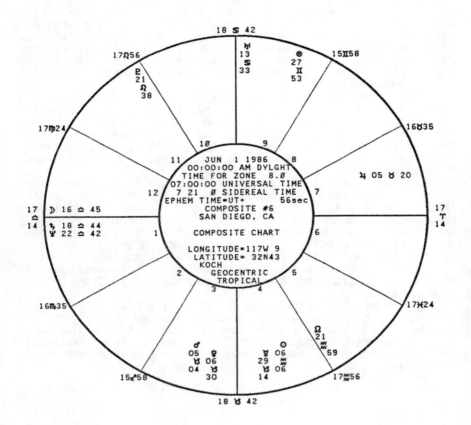

Composite Chart 6

170

There are many indications of a strong love for and mutual support of one another in this composite. Among them are the conjunctions of the Ascendant and Descendant rulers, the MC/NADIR rulers, Mars/Venus and Moon/Saturn/Ascendant. Jupiter in the 7th House describes the expansion they derive from being together along with the work they do with others. They are both healers, metaphysicians and artists, and like to share every aspect of their individual lives with each other.

Their meeting with each other produced a strong feeling that they had been together before. There was an instant recognition, which is not uncommon with conjunctions such as Moon/Ascendant, Moon/Saturn, Moon/Neptune and South Node/Pluto. But there are lessons as well. The Moon/Saturn/Neptune cluster on the Ascendant squares Uranus and the parental 4th/10th axis. With strong Saturn aspects, they are learning effective time management and organization. They are also learning to respond spontaneously to the feelings they have for each other rather than holding back or controlling their feelings based on preconceived role models (Moon/Saturn). That strong Saturn says they can be serious too much of the time, so they are also learning how to play and have fun. But the seriousness of it all doesn't seem to phase them - "We are often amazed and feel blessed at the continual growth and strength of our love for one another and the harmony that we experience on all levels."

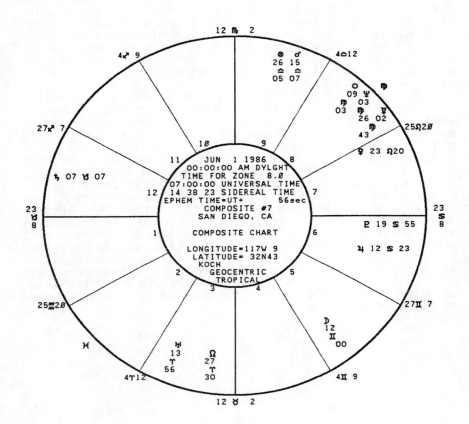

Composite Chart 7

172

After 32 years of marriage and raising four children together, this couple says any problem areas have all pretty much worked themselves out. The elements are there for marriage and family. A 7th House partnership oriented Venus ruling the 4th House (family) and a 5th house children oriented Moon seem to be pretty good indications of this. The Sun is square the Moon, an indication of two distinct personalities coming together to work out what-ever challenges exist between what is expressed outwardly and what is felt inwardly (Sun-outer, Moon-inner).

A Virgo Sun conjunct Mercury and Neptune trine Saturn would seem to describe one personality. This strong earth trine is well suited for work, business and financial success. The Gemini Moon trine Mars in the 9th brings in philosophy, education and travel as the other driving force in the relationship. They met at college and the attraction was instant (Ascendant ruler Saturn squaring Mars for attraction in 9/12 for educational surrounding).

A grand cross in cardinal signs involves Uranus, Mars, Jupiter and Saturn. Many ups and downs would be experienced over the years with this kind of potent energy operating in the chart. Other challenges inherent in the cardinal cross include wanting to do it all. Aries asks, "Are my needs being met?", while Libra asks, "Is my partner satisfied?" Cancer wants to take care of domestic longings, while Capricorn's focus is the job and profession. These issues are common themes for the professional couple that is also raising a family.

With Jupiter in Cancer in the 6th House, their joint expansion would come through the family and service given to the family.

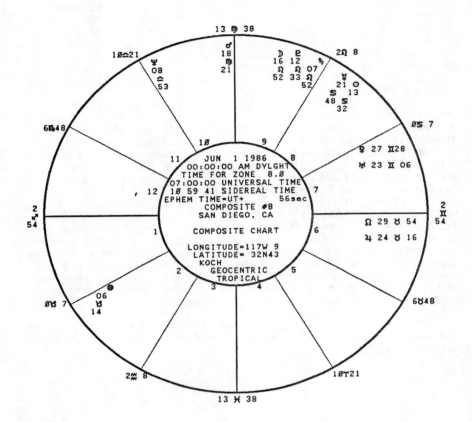

Composite Chart 8

The attraction was not what you'd call instant in this case. They knew each other for 17 years before they decided to get married, each being a friend of the family's. When they did decide to get married, Uranus was transiting the composite Ascendant.

The family ties are shown by Sun and Mercury in Cancer, as well as the Nodes contacting the Ascendant/Descendant. With both signs Cancer and Leo prominent as well as 4th and 5th House rulers elevated in the 10th House, their goal is to raise children, animals and plants.

Both partners feel a strong need for home and security. They both have a creative nature and enjoy the same artistic forms of entertainment, such as theater, dance and music. Both love to teach.

The personalities are quite different. The Sun in Cancer and Mars in Virgo describe the male aspect of this relationship. He is quite content to be at home, read, study, do programming, analysis and work around the house. Venus conjunct Uranus in Gemini plus Moon in Leo conjunct Pluto would describe the female aspect of this relationship. She, while loving the home, also seeks enjoyment and stimulation from socializing with people, going to parties, travel and a variety of different hobbies. With an elevated Moon conjunct Pluto in Leo, it is also quite easy for her to "run the show." The North Node conjunct the Descendant is teaching them both how to give in a relationship.

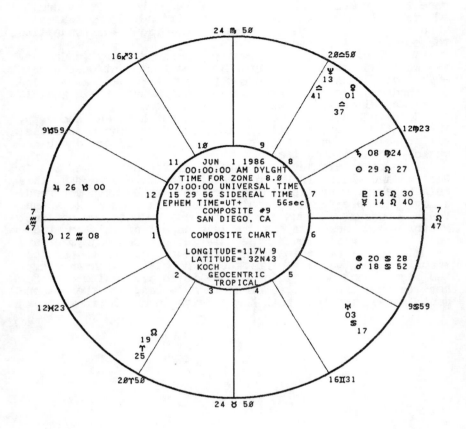

Composite Chart 9

176

The Leo/Aquarius polarity is dominant in this composite with a Leo Sun and Aquarius Moon and Ascendant. This couple has been together seven years and have continuously sought to balance that Aquarian need for freedom and detachment with Leo's needs for closeness and affection. A subemphasis in the chart is Libra (three planets in the sign, four in the house), which does blend well with Leo and Aquarius to bring about sharing and equality as strong themes of the relationship.

There is a strong "togetherness" theme in this composite, with all the activity centered around the Descendant (Sun, Mercury and Pluto). Saturn in a 7th House composite, contrary to myth, usually indicates a long lasting relationship, one that endures through time. The lesson with it in the 7th in Virgo involves a tendency both partners have of expecting perfection from the other and of being too critical.

When they're not working (which is almost always with Saturn in Virgo and Mars in the 6th House), they are pursuing joint hobbies, creative interests and home entertaining (Ascendant ruler in Cancer in the 5th).

The thing they seem to be learning to deal with the most is the handling of money (Nodes in 2nd and 8th). Their privacy and intimacy with each other is one of their priorities with Jupiter in the 12th and Venus/ Neptune in the 8th. Lovemaking tends to be a heightened spiritual experience with Venus, Neptune and the South Node in Libra in the 8th House. Their children are computers, astrology, and audio and visual electronic equipment. (Uranus in the 5th, Aquarius rising, Moon in Aquarius).

Pluto's aspect to the Ascendant/Descendant axis indicates the powerful level at which this couple interacts. Its opposition to the Moon identifies the emotional ups and downs they have experienced and how they've been a transformative force to each other. At the time of their marriage, a 5-planet stellium in Leo including the Sun, Moon, Mercury, Venus and Jupiter all contacted the 7th House of this composite chart and the planets therein.

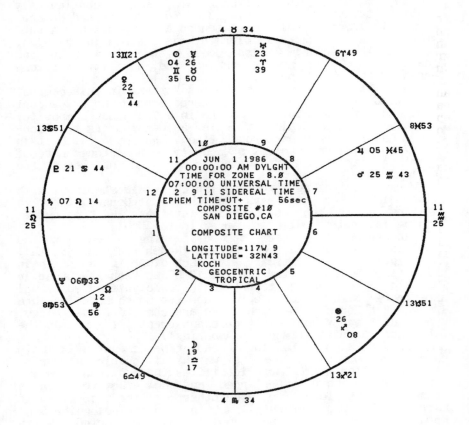

Composite Chart 10

They met through a working situation (Ascendant ruler in the 10th) and felt an instant attraction for each other. A feeling of recognition swept through them - "I know you from somewhere." At the time of meeting, Mercury, Venus and Neptune transited the Part of Fortune in the 5th House while Uranus transited 5 degrees Sagittarius, making a grand cross out of the mutable T-square involving the Sun, Jupiter and Neptune.

They both recognize that they are strong personalities and have life styles and patterns that seem at odds with each other. This is partially shown by the two T-squares - one involving the Sun (him) and the other involving the Moon (her). The fact that Uranus was transiting the Sun's T-square at the time of meeting also acknowledges the radical changes that were occurring for him at that time. She came to offer support, care and attention and before long, they were deeply involved.

She is described by the T-square with the Moon, Uranus and Pluto, and struggles fiercely to maintain independence and commitment to a cause. Many T-squares involving Pluto also imply the necessity of letting something or someone else go in order to have this relationship. This was necessary for her as she found herself saying good-bye to a lover of many years, and a business partner and job that could not tolerate her newfound love.

He is described by the T-square involving the Sun, Jupiter and Neptune, suggesting a somewhat idealized vision of what a partner should be and do. The outlet in the 4th House points to the home as the point of fulfillment.

When it comes to romance and love, they fulfill each other's longings as no one has previously. The grand trine involving Moon, Mars and Venus attests to this.

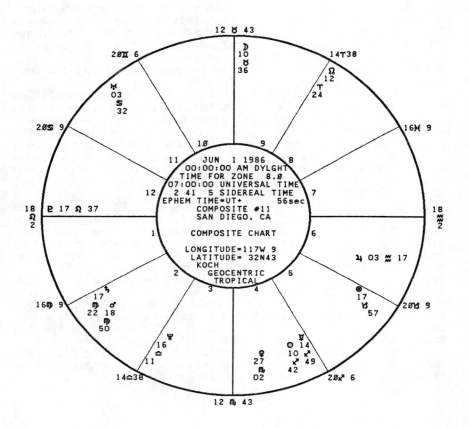

Composite Chart 11

This is a good example of many inconjuncts (the 150 degree aspect) as it applies to composites. In a natal chart, inconjuncts often reveal two foreign elements trying to integrate totally different attitudes each parent holds, trying to be unified and integrated in the child. In a composite, it concerns two people trying to integrate and unify a diverse set of backgrounds or attitudes and make it work.

In this chart, the Moon inconjuncts the Sun, Mercury, South Node and Neptune. Different family backgrounds and a big socio-economic class difference exists between these two. The Moon is elevated in Taurus - she came from wealth and high society. There was a lot of pressure exerted upon him to be a good provider, "to measure up." Money - who earns and provides - eventually became the destroyer with 4th House planets Sun and Mercury square 2nd House cusp planets Saturn and Mars. The Nodes (a frequent indicator of what needs to be worked out and where the growth will take place) are positioned in the 2nd/8th, involving contrasting values and monetary differences.

Family background plays a large part in this composite, with emphasis on 4th House planets and the ASC ruler in the 4th. The fact that the 4th House planets inconjunct the Moon in the 9th could be troublesome for domestic harmony and relations with in-laws.

The 9th House is also a travel house and the inconjunct to the 4th House (roots and home) often indicates an adjustment or balance has to be arrived at between how much time is spent in or away from the home. His work required much out of town travel so there were many periods of separation for them (Jupiter/6th inconjunct Uranus/11th). Still, it was quite a romantic relationship for most of the 7 years they remained together.

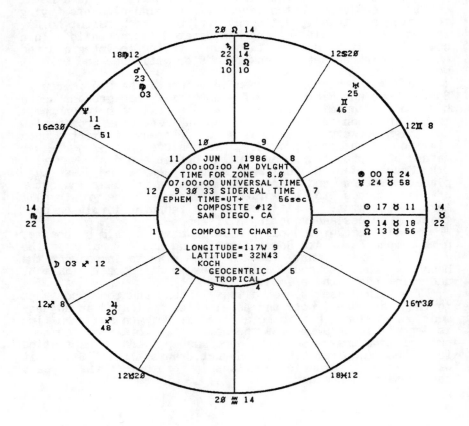

Composite Chart 12

How did they meet? Doing radical political work in college in 1969 (Ascendant ruler Pluto in the 9th). A very intense attraction occurred which is typical with an active Mars or Pluto. In this case they're both active; Pluto squares the 7th House stellium and Mars is the focal point of a T-square in the mutable mode.

A packed 7th House...Sun conjunct Venus...the Nodes sitting along the Ascendant/Descendant axis...a seemingly perfect relationship, right? But wait. As we look closer at that 7th House stellium, we find a lot of pressure coming from Saturn and Pluto squares. The Saturn square says, "This is how I expect you to behave and conform." The Pluto square says, "Let me remold you the way I want you."

He was supportive of her, cheered her on and raised her spirits (Moon in Sagittarius in the 1st), but no aspects to the Moon left her feeling somehow not really involved with him and his life. They could really talk (Mercury trine Mars), but also misinterpreted where the other was coming from (Mercury square Saturn). His inability to "tell the whole truth" (Sun inconjunct Neptune) made her open, honest Moon in Sagittarius approach to the relationship difficult. He fit her picture of "the one" but she didn't fit his. She was okay for a lover, but not a permanent mate (Uranus, Mars and Jupiter mutable T-square).

They tried off and on to reunite over the years, rekindling the fiery attraction described by the Pluto in this chart, but neither one would allow the other the total control that the Saturn/Pluto squares dictate.

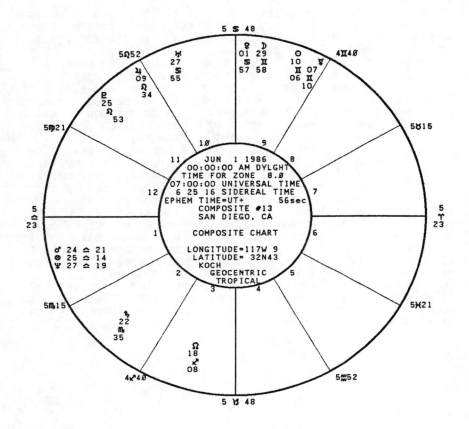

Composite Chart 13

Libra is rising - they were introduced by a mutual friend. The Ascendant ruler Venus is in Cancer conjunct the Moon - an excellent indicator of cohabitational compatibility. They wound up becoming romantically involved and living together.

A 9th House stellium gives emphasis to the philosophical outlook they shared together, along with a love of travel. The Moon/Venus conjunction shows the love, nurturing and caring they felt for each other. When one party was recovering from an accident, the other became like a parent and vice versa.

One of the most challenging aspects of this composite couple involves Pluto square Saturn in the 2nd House. That potent type of energy in a square can indicate bottled up tension and frustration seeking release in a volatile way. With Saturn in the 2nd House, one of the lessons may deal with the issue of personal values and money: who earns what, how much is spent and so forth. This has been one issue that has caused some turmoil in their relationship and they are aware that it needs constant attention so that it doesn't get out of hand.

Uranus in the 10th squares Mars and Neptune in the 1st. This says a great deal about who they are as a couple and their image in the world. Parental re-programming involving what is traditional in a relationship and what is not is an issue they have had to deal with because as a gay couple, their relationship challenges tradition.

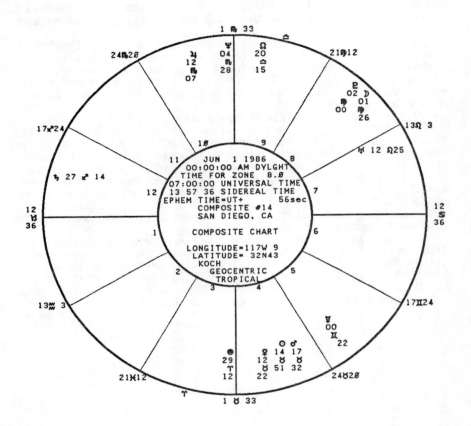

Composite Chart 14

This was a powerful, magnetic, instant attraction (Uranus inconjunct the Ascendant), but there are uncontrollable forces at work here (the inconjunct). Many differences in background and attitudes must be worked out as stated by all the inconjuncts in this chart.

Capricorn rises – they are both ambitious and love their work. Uranus occupies the 7th House – they are mutually understanding of needing personal freedom. The Sun conjuncts Mars and Venus – they are awed and held spellbound by the compulsive love and passion which exists between them. They are both compulsive in love (Moon conjunct Pluto).

Separation and long distance communication is a problem that results in an "out of sight, out of mind" complex (Mercury in Gemini square a Moon/Pluto conjunction in Virgo). They also have an exact square from Venus to Uranus, an aspect that usually suggests a strong attraction and magnetism alternated with sudden bursts of freedom and separation.

They both are equally captivated by and enamored of one another, what with the Moon/Pluto conjunction in the 8th House and the Sun/Mars/Venus conjunction in the 4th. An exact T-square between Venus, Jupiter and Uranus makes this relationship exciting, unpredictible, adventurous and loving.

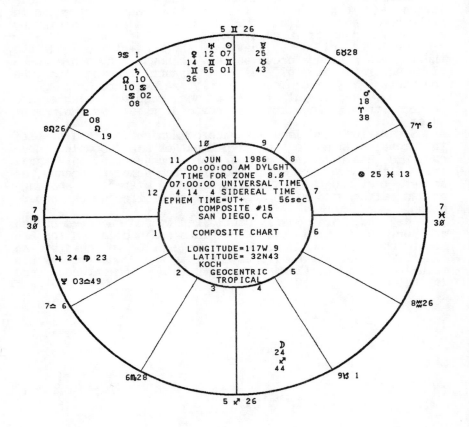

Composite Chart 15

This relationship has been on again/off again an incredible number of times during its eight year history. This is largely due to the fact that unpredictible, restless Uranus holds such a position of prominence in the composite chart. Its conjunction to the Sun, Venus and MC (in mutable Gemini) would seem to be enough to handle, but its exact square to the Ascendant/Descendant makes this relationship seem even less stable. So what is holding it together at all?

The traditional concept of Uranus deals with freedom, rebellion, unpredictibility and willfulness. But there is a side of Uranus that is electrically charged with attraction and magnetism as well. With the Venus/Uranus conjunction, there is a powerful attraction that works like a magnet. It draws the two together when they are apart, but can also create static electricity when they are together, forcing them to get some room to breathe.

There are a lot of mutable signs prominent in this chart, including the Sun, Moon and angles. The mutable mode tends to need a lot of change and variety.

A Saturn/North Node conjunction and the South Node in Saturn's sign deals with lessons they've chosen to work out together. This combination can tend toward moodiness and depression, even though it is great for working together as a team and learning from one another.

Chapter 6

THE TIME/SPACE CHART

DEFINITION AND CALCULATIONS
OF THE TIME/SPACE CHART

A relationship chart, like a composite chart, pulls
together two distinct units into one whole. The basic difference is that a relationship chart is based on a time/
space midpoint rather than a planetary midpoint. Thus, the
spacial midpoint of longitude between someone born at 90W12
and one born at 87W55 would be 89W03. The spacial midpoint
of latitude between someone born at 38N38 and one born at
43N02 would be 40N50. To arrive at the time midpoint, the
same procedure is used, as follows.

CHART A: JULY 6, 1954,   11:14 PM
CHART B: OCTOBER 8, 1954,   4:20 PM
MIDPOINT: AUGUST 22, 1954,   7:47 PM

Thus, a new chart is calculated for August 22, 1954 at
7:47 PM, 40N50, 89W03. This kind of chart calculation is
best left to a computer or computer service because it involves tedious mathematics. On charts from Astro Computing
Services, the Julian Date may be consulted for greater ease
in determining midpoint dates. The Julian Date is also
listed in the American Ephemeris for the 20th Century (Michelson, 1980).

INTERPRETATION OF THE TIME/SPACE CHART

The interpretation of this chart is identical to that
of the composite chart. Often, the two charts look similar, but they do have distinct differences. For example, a
recent comparison of the two showed the composite chart to
have Cancer rising while the relationship chart had a 4th
House Sun and planets.
Timing transits and progressions to these charts are

191

quite effective. They may yield different statements, but arrive at the same answers. The only confusion that will arise in working with these two charts is trying to mix them. Apples and oranges do not mix. Astrology is symbolic and a multitude of systems will work that utilize this symbology. The confusion arises when we attempt to look at different systems and work with them simultaneously. The best plan is to choose the system or comparison method you like best and work with it consistently. Then you will see everything makes sense.

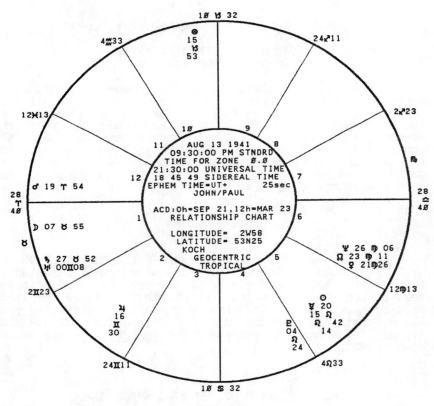

Figure 6-1

**The Time/Space Chart of
John Lennon and Paul McCartney**

Figure 6-1 is the Relationship chart of John Lennon and Paul McCartney. For reference and comparison, their com-

192

posite chart is Figure 5-2 in Chapter 5. What are the similarities from the relationship chart to the composite chart and what are the differences? Why would you use one over another? Can you use both? Let's look at these issues, one by one.

A great many similarities exist between the Composite Chart (Figure 5-2) and the Time/Space Chart (Figure 6-1) of Lennon and McCartney. Both charts have Aries rising, 5th House Leo Suns and similar house placements for all the planets. In fact, there are only a few differences. One is that in the composite chart, the Moon is placed in the 7th House at 7 degrees Scorpio, while in the Time/Space chart it is in the 1st House at 7 degrees Taurus. It squares Pluto in both charts, an aspect that ultimately led to the separation of these two. In both cases, the Moon square Pluto can indicate a question of values, control and dominating power struggles. It is also an aspect that gave depth and character to their relationship and their creations, allowing them to continually transform and regenerate themselves.

The theme that appears clear in both charts is the vast amount of resources, talent and wealth that became available to them. Both charts contain strong earth and fire, a combination that, among other things, is known for its incredible ability to generate creative ideas and make them work. The fire element is the creative spark of spontaneity and enthusiasm while the earth element is practical, organized and accomplished. Together, the two elements can be very successful in the material world. In fact, this is probably the best use of fire and earth together - a creative relationship that comes together to make money and get things accomplished, because the two elements can create a lot of friction together, and if not channeled properly, could be very destructive towards one another.

The Time/Space chart also contains a nicely placed Venus in Virgo, in conjunction to Neptune and the North Node. This is an outstanding aspect for musicians, artists and those promoting love. Its placement in Virgo, trining Saturn, also indicates a potentially well run business organization.

Probably a good rule of thumb in comparing the two charts for strong statements is locating patterns that appear in both. Both charts have the Sun/Saturn square and both have the Moon/Pluto square. These aspects both have the tendency to create a powerful attraction and intense relationship with one another, but they also have the tendency to become volatile and are not often permanent in nature. And yet, looking at what these two accomplished with each other in the short time that they were together is more than enough to compensate for the lack of stability in their relationship. What they created with each other, their 5th House progeny, will endure through time.

As I mentioned earlier, I prefer using a composite chart to analyze a relationship, but this is truly a matter of personal preference. Whichever you're more comfortable with is the one you should use, and many people use both.

The one advantage a relationship chart has over a composite chart is the ease with which you can progress it. Unlike the composite, the relationship chart does have a birth-date, time and place and this makes progressions easy to do. To progress a composite, on the other hand, you must first progress the two individual charts and then compute the composite planets and houses from that.

Although progressions and transits have not been cov-ered in this book, those that work with them will find even more helpful data when using them in composite and rela-tionship astrology. The basic composite or time/space chart will describe the couple and how they interact, where-as the transits or progressions will point to timing fac-tors and help point out specific issues that are in focus. But that is a subject for another book.

RESEARCH ON COUPLES

In Chapter 3, Section 3 "Planet-to-Planet Contacts between Charts" several references were made to frequently or infrequently found aspects among long-term married couples or short-term couples. These references are based on research done at ISAR (International Society for Astrological Research) in March, 1984.

Research Methodology

Two groups of relationships were analyzed, both in reference to each other and to a group of controls. The first group consisted of 106 pairs of Long-Term Couples (LT). To qualify as an LT, the couple would have been married for a minimum of 10 years. The second group consisted of 145 pairs of Short-Term Couples (ST). The ST group, some still married, others not, have been together less than 10 years.

Twenty-one planets and points were examined. These included: Sun, Moon, Mercury, Venus, Mars, Ceres, Pallas, Juno, Vesta, Jupiter, Saturn, Chiron, Uranus, Neptune, Pluto, True (North) Node, Mean (South) Node, Anti-vertex, East Point, Ascendant and Midheaven. Eighteen different aspects were tallied. These included: conjunction, square, opposition, trine and inconjunct (3 degree orb); sextile, octile and trioctile (2 degree orb); and semi-sextile, quintile, bi-quintile, decile, bi-novile, novile, tri-septile, bi-septile, quatri-novile and septile (1 degree orb).

A program was written by Mark Pottenger to tally the angular separations of each of the aforementioned aspects. The same tallies were used for the Control Group. The Control Group consisted of charts from within the test group which were mixed to produce randomly derived couples. Tallies exist for each individual aspect, along with tallies of Hard aspects (conjunction, square, opposition, octile, tri-octile); Ptolemaic aspects (conjunction, opposition, trine, square, sextile) and All aspects.

Once both the test group and control group tallies were completed, a chi-square test was applied to determine significance of any of these aspects. Certain aspects were expected to be significant while other aspects were expected to be the reverse before the chi-square was performed. Because so many aspects were found to be of significance in the test group, those that have been cited in this text are limited to 0.005 level of significance with 1 degree of freedom.

In the LT group, the chi-square value of what was significant in the test group far exceeded the chi-square value of what was significant for the control group.

The results of these tests are by no means final. They

need to be analyzed aspect-by-aspect and planet-by-planet and this work is still in process. There will be test runs of other degree orbs as well, for instance, widening the orb of the conjunction and narrowing and perhaps even eliminating some of the other aspects.

Those who wish to examine the data may do so by contacting the author in care of the publisher.

DATA COLLECTION

MICK JAGGER
7/26/1943
6:30 AM DBST
Dartford, England
51N27 0E12
ABC

PRINCE CHARLES
11/13/1948
9:14 PM GST
London, England
51N31 0W06
ABC

PRINCESS DIANA
7/1/1961
7:45 PM GDT
London, England
51N31 0W06
LMR

ELIZABETH TAYLOR
2/27/1932
7:56 PM GST
London, England
51N31 0W06
PW

RICHARD BURTON
11/10/1925
7:58 PM GST
Pontrhydfen, Wales
52N17 3W51
ABC-DD

PAUL NEWMAN
1/26/1925
6:30 AM EST
Cleveland, OH
41N30 81W42
ABC

JOANN WOODWARD
2/27/1930
4:00 AM EST
Thomasville, GA
30N50 83W59
PW/errata sheet

U.S.A.
7/4/1776
2:13 AM LMT
Philadelphia, PA
39N57 75W08
HSC

U.S.S.R.
11/7/1917
10:52 PM LMT
Lenningrad, Russia
59N56 30E24
BWH

F. D. ROOSEVELT
1/30/1882
8:45 PM EST
Hyde Parkn NY
41N48 73W56
PC; SS

JOHN LENNON
10/9/1940
6:30 PM GST
Liverpool, England
53N25 2W58
LMR

PAUL McCARTNEY
6/18/1942
2:30 AM DBST
Liverpool, England
53N25 2W58
ABC-DD; PC

PAUL SIMON
10/13/1941
2:33 AM EST
New York, NY
40N45 73W57
LMR

ARTHUR GARFUNKEL
11/5/1941
11:00 PM EST
New York, NY
40N45 73W57
ABC-DD; PC

ABC   – American Book of Charts "A" or "B" Data
ABC-DD – American Book of Charts "Dirty Data"
BWH   – Book of World Horoscopes
HSC   – Horoscopes of the U.S. States and Cities
LMR   – Lois M. Rodden
PC   – Penfield Collection
PW   – Profiles of Women
SS   – Sabian Symbols

BIBLIOGRAPHY AND RECOMMENDED READING

The American Atlas. Compiled and programmed by Thomas G. Shanks. San Diego: Astro Computing Services, 1978.

Arroyo, Stephen. Astrology, Karma and Transformation. Davis, CA: CRCS Publications, 1978.

Arroyo, Stephen. Relationships & Life Cycles. Vancouver, WA: CRCS Publications, 1979.

ASTRO*CARTO*GRAPHY by Jim Lewis. San Francisco, CA: 1976.

Bills, Rex E. The Rulership Book, A Directory of Astrological Correspondences. Richmond, VA: Macoy Publishing & Masonic Supply Co., Inc., 1971.

Dodson, Carolyn R. Horoscopes of the U.S. States & Cities. Pelham, NY: Astro Computing Services, 1975.

Ebertin, Reinhold. The Combination of Stellar Influences. Tempe, AZ: American Federation of Astrologers, Inc., 1940. Reprint: 1972

Ferguson, Marilyn. The Aquarian Conspiracy: Personal & Social Transformation in the 1980's. Los Angeles: J. P. Tarcher, Inc., 1980.

Gauquelin, Michel. Cosmic Influences on Human Behavior. New York: ASI Publishers Inc., 1978.

Greene, Liz. Relating: An Astrological Guide to Living with Others on a Small Planet. New York: Samuel Weiser, Inc., 1978.

Guttman, Gail. "Planetary Cycles of Marriage and Divorce". KOSMOS Quarterly Journal, Vol. XII No. 4, Fall 1983.

-----. "Relationship Study". KOSMOS Quarterly Journal, Vol. XIV No. 2 (Spring 1985).

Hand, Robert. Horoscope Symbols. Rockport, MA: Para Research, 1981.

-----. Planets in Composite. Rockport, MA: Para Research, 1975.

Jansky, Robert. Horoscopes: Here and Now. Van Nuys, CA: Astro-Analytics, 1974. Reprint: 1976.

Jones, Marc Edmund. The Sabian Symbols in Astrology. Boulder, CO: Shambala Publications, Inc., 1953. Reprint: 1969.

Larousse Encyclopedia of Astrology. Compiled by Jean-Louis Brau, Helen Weaver, and Allan Edmands, 1977. New York: McGraw-Hill Book Company, 1980.

Mann, A. T. The Round Art, The Astrology of Time & Space. Copyright Dragon's World Ltd., 1979. New York: Mayflower Books, Inc.

Michelson, Neil F. The American Ephemeris for the 20th Century. San Diego: Astro Computing Services, 1980.

Moore, Moon. The Book of World Horoscopes. Birmingham, MI: Seek-It-Publications, 1980.

Morrison, Al H. and J. Lee Lehman. Ephemeris of Amor, Eros and Sappho. New York: CAO Times, 1980.

Murstein, Bernard I. Love, Sex & Marriage through the Ages. New York: Springer Publishing Company, Inc., 1974.

Penfield, Marc. 2001: The Penfield Collection. Seattle: Vulcan Books, 1979.

Dean, Geoffrey and Arthur Mather. Recent Advances in Natal Astrology. Bromley, Kent, England: The Astrological Association, 1977.

Rodden, Lois M. The American Book of Charts. San Diego: Astro Computing Services, 1980.

------. The Mercury Method of Chart Comparison.

------. Profiles of Women. Tempe, AZ: American Federation of Astrologers, Inc., 1979.

Thorsten, Geraldine. God Herself: The Feminine Roots of Astrology. New York: Avon Books, 1980.

U. S. Bureau of the Census. Statistical Abstract of the United States: 1982-83 (103rd edition). Washington D.C.: 1982.

Zunin, Leonard, MD. Contact: The First Four Minutes. New York: Ballantine Books, 1972. Reprint: 1981.

BIBLIOGRAPHY OF SONGS

Benjamin, Bennie, Sol Marcus and Gloria Caldwell. "DON'T LET ME BE MISUNDERSTOOD". Bennie Benjamin Music, Inc., copyright 1964, 1965.

Brooks, Joe. "YOU LIGHT UP MY LIFE". New York: Big Hill Music Corp., copyright 1976, 1977.

Browne, Jackson and Glenn Frey. "TAKE IT EASY". WB Music Corp., copyright 1972.

Croce, Jim. "I'LL HAVE TO SAY I LOVE YOU IN A SONG". New York: Blendingwell Musick Corp. Inc. , copyright 1973, 1974.

Henley, Don and Glenn Frey. "DESPERADO". New York: WB Music Corp. and Kicking Bear Music, copyright 1973.

Jagger, Mick and Keith Richards. "YOU CAN'T ALWAYS GET WHAT YOU WANT". New York: Abkco Musci, Inc., copyright 1969.

King, Carole. "WILL YOU LOVE ME TOMORROW". Hollywood, CA: Screen Gems-EMI Music, Inc., copyright 1960, 1961.

Kipner, Stephen A. and Terry Shaddick. "PHYSICAL". New York: April Music, Inc., Ajpril/Blackwood Publications, copyright 1981.

Lake, Greg. "LUCKY MAN" New York: Tro, Cotillion.
Lennon, John and Paul McCartney. "WHEN I'M SIXTY-FOUR". Hollywood, CA: Norhtern Songs, Ltd., Maclen Music, Inc., copyright 1967.

Loggins, Kenny and Melissa Manchester. "WHENEVER I CALL YOU FRIEND". New York: Milk Money Music, Inc. and Rumanian Pickleworks, copyright 1978.

Loggins, Kenny and Michael McDonald. "WHAT A FOOL BELIEVES". New York: Milk Money Music, Inc. and Snug Music, copyright 1978.

MacColl, Ewan. "THE FIRST TIME EVER I SAW YOUR FACE". New York: Stormking Music Inc., Music Sales Corp., copyright 1962, 1966, 1972.

MacDonald, Ralph, William Salter and Bill Withers. "JUST THE TWO OF US". Antisia Music, Inc., copyright 1980.

McVie,Christine. "OVER MY HEAD". Fleetwood Mac Music, Warner Tamberlane Publishing Co., copyright 1975.

Mitchell, Joni. "HELP ME". Beverly Hills, CA: Crazy Crow Music, copyright 1973, 1974.

Mitchell, Joni. "BOTH SIDES NOW". Beverly Hills, CA: Siquomb Music, Inc., copyright 1967, 1973.

Morrison, Van. "MOONDANCE" by Van Morrison. New York: copyright 1970 & 1971.

Nash, Graham. "CHICAGO". Brtoken Birk Music (BMI) from SD7204 "Songs for Beginners", copyright 1971.

Nicks, Stevie. "DREAMS". Los Angeles: Gentoo Music, Inc. and Welsh Witch Music, copyright 1977.

Rundgren, Todd. "LOVE IS THE ANSWER". Earmark Music, Inc./Fiction Music, Inc. (BMI), copyright 1977.

Tempchin, Jack. "PEACEFUL EASY FEELING". WB Music Corp. and Jazz Bird Music, copyright 1972.

Woolfson, Eric and Alan Parsons. "TIME". Wollfsons Ltd./Careers Music, Inc., copyright 1979.